WILKINSON

WILKINSON

Warrior, Musician, Bishop

George Young

Anglican Book Centre
Toronto, Ontario

1984
Anglican Book Centre
600 Jarvis Street
Toronto, Ontario
Canada M4Y 2J6

Printed and bound in Canada by John Deyell Company

Canadian Cataloguing in Publication Data

Young, George, 1916-
  Wilkinson
Includes index.
ISBN 0-919891-17-9 (bound) (pbk.)
1. Wilkinson, Frederick Hugh, 1986-
2. Bishops - Canada - Biography. I. Title.
BX5620.W54Y 68 1984   283′.092′4   C84-099236-X

His life was gentle, and the elements so mix'd in him that Nature might stand up and say to all the world, "This was a man."

William Shakespeare

CONTENTS

FOREWORD

This is an unusual biography in that it portrays at one time the lives of two notable Canadians.

First and foremost is the subject of the book himself, the late Fred Wilkinson, courageous citizen-soldier in World War I, lifelong musician and organist, strong and compassionate leader in Canada and abroad among Anglican clergymen, counsellor and friend to thousands, devoted husband and father, and no mean cook. More formally described, he is the Right Reverend Frederick Hugh Wilkinson, MM and bars, ED, MA, BD, DD, LLD, DCL (honoris causa), STD (honoris causa), and was Bishop of the Anglican Diocese of Toronto.

The second life, which emerges unobtrusively but necessarily, is that of the author himself, Canon George V. Young, also an Anglican clergyman in the Diocese of Toronto and a citizen-soldier but veteran of World War II. He was widely known in Toronto as the rector of St Anne's Anglican Church, a centre of religious art and music, housed in a beautiful Byzantine building, the only one in the city, which George had rescued from improvident sale and nursed back to orthodox splendor.

George Young's additional relevance to his present role, and the reason for his being asked and undertaking to write the Wilkinson history, was his unusually close friendship with Fred and the confidence that each had in the other, a sort of

Doctor Johnson and Boswell relationship. It began when Fred was Bishop and George a rector in the same diocese, but blossomed later, during the fruitful years between Fred's retirement as bishop and his death in 1980.

In these mature years Fred became a patriarchal figure in Canada, a sort of confessor, counsellor, companion, and host to countless friends, and chaplain and "visitor" to many groups, religious, military, civic, educational, and social. As I observed, Canon Young was with him often at this time. Occasionally I was included in their lunch-time discussions and in special events at St Anne's Church.

In any event, I was already a close friend and admirer of the Bishop and Mrs Wilkinson, as was my wife. She and our daughters were all his parishioners when he was the rector at St Paul's Anglican Church, Bloor Street. It was then that he assisted me in making an easy transition from the United Church of Canada of my forbears to the Anglican Church in Canada, and so to full communion with my wife and children.

Consequently, as a friend of Fred, the subject, and George, the author, I am able and happy to commend both the subject and the authenticity of his biography, as well as to understand the author's enthusiasm in writing it. The book is a very knowledgeable account of a truly great Canadian and a Christian, well worthy of the many honours bestowed upon him in his lifetime, and the affection and respect with which he is now remembered.

Without anticipating what follows I am glad to think that those who read further, whatever their calling and interests, will find much of interest and inspiration in Dr Wilkinson's life, as recounted by his Boswell.

The Rt Hon Roland Michener
former Governor-General of Canada

PREFACE

It was a year ago that Dr Reginald Stackhouse, the principal of Wycliffe College, came to visit me in Florida. After lunch we set out along the beach, and as we walked he rehearsed the reasons why I should write a biography of Bishop Wilkinson. While I agreed that I had known the bishop better than many, I did not feel I was capable of doing justice to the subject. Some weeks went by before Reg Stackhouse returned again, this time accompanied by Jimmy Traviss, a leading layman and friend of the bishop. Once again the subject was raised, and finally, I agreed to tackle it. But I agreed with great trepidation, remembering the remark of the Right Honourable Roland Michener at the unveiling of the bishop's portrait: "It would require a Boswell to record his many achievements and accomplishments."

Bishop Wilkinson was, I believe, one of the most extraordinary men. Supremely gifted, he was the chairman of the board, the sensitive artist in performance, the warm and understanding cleric, the sincere and humble worshipper, and the strong and steady leader of his flock. Every role in his long career he played superbly. He personified authority balanced by an enormous sense of humanity. It is fitting that such a life should be set down in print for those coming after him.

The work has been hampered by the fact that the bishop left no notes or personal papers. At the repeated urging of myself and others, he said he had begun to write down some aspects of his life; but I have been unable to find the notes. An added problem was the demise of so many of his collegues before him; his times in western Canada and Montreal are correspondingly lean.

There is an old saying: "Give the best you have and make no apologies." This is what I have tried to do, trusting the reader will discover in these pages that unselfishness, kindness, and integrity are still to be found, and that the possessor of such virtues does sometimes rise to the top.

PROLOGUE

The setting is the beautiful gothic style edifice of the Cathedral Church of St James, mother church of the Anglican Diocese of Toronto. The nave is crowded with people from all walks of life, representatives of the national, provincial, and municipal governments, heads of other faiths and denominations, musicians, artists, and choral scholars, leaders of the judicial and medical professions, members of the loyal and fraternal societies, row upon row of robed clergy, and resplendent in full dress uniform, members of the armed forces. In the chancel between the robed choir rests the catafalque, and on it the earthly remains of he whom all have come this day to honour — Frederick Hugh Wilkinson, warrior, musician, bishop, and seventh occupant of the see of Toronto.

He planned the service himself. There was to be no eulogy, only the burial office of the Prayer Book, which has been read over king and commoner for four centuries. His choosing the ninetieth psalm "Lord Thou has been our refuge," as well as the hymn "The King of Love My Shepherd is," was consistent with his favorite theme: the providence of God in the life of man. This he lived and believed with passionate conviction, and to all who knew him this would be the last message he wanted to leave.

He requested that the words of St John be included; they were read by Bishop Snell: "He that overcometh shall inherit all things; and I will be his God, and he shall be my son." In the silence that followed, these words seemed to speak the thoughts of all present. One of his favorite hymns "For all the Saints" was sung. The creed and prayers followed, and an anthem, the blessing, and the resurrection hymn "Jesus lives, thy terrors now" brought the service to a close.

The Archbishop of Toronto led the coffin out of the cathedral, flanked by ten brother bishops, honorary pallbearers, and outside an honour guard of the Queen's Own Rifles, the Canadian Corp of Commissionaires, and the Boy Scouts. To a piper's lament the bishop's body was laid to rest beside the grave of his beloved wife, in the grounds of St Johns Anglican Church, York Mills. Mournfully a bugle sounded the last post; the last call had been answered and the job well done.

It was a funeral service, but it was also a witness of the heights to which the human spirit can soar. What else would bring so many to pay honour to this man who had for some thirteen years been out of public office, and who at the age of 83 had seen so many of his contemporaries precede him in death? Seldom does one out of the main stream of public life draw such a large and diverse gathering of people in a testimony of tribute and esteem. As he wished, there had been no public eulogy, but there were countless unspoken ones; for each who knew him at some stage in his long life of service had rich memories of the warmth, kindness, and generosity of this great man. One old comrade fondly remembered the modest and very young enlisted man in France who was to become a hero in World War I and had been cited on three distinct occasions for bravery. Some remembered the same young man who after the war gave superb recitals on the great organ in Convocation Hall during his student days at University College. One spoke of the way he made the Old Testament come alive for his students at Emmanuel College in Saskatoon. Many remembered his rich ministry to his congregations in Calgary, Vancouver, Montreal, and Toronto, the wisdom he imparted and the pastoral care and concern he showed. Many more in those cities, whose lives he touched and influenced for good entirely outside the Anglican Church, treasured the memory of his ecumenical leadership and his warm friendship for other denominations and faiths.

Leaders of industry and men of business who worked with him acclaimed his organizing ability and administrative skill in his church extension work, which saw the establishment of seventy new parishes and churches, or in his hosting of bishops, priests, laymen, from every Anglican diocese in the world at the Anglican Congress in 1963. The clergy had good reason to remember him. He was always accessible; he invited them to receptions and conferences, anticipated their needs and frustrations, and was always ready with a portion of his courage and a cheque in need.

These and countless memories will be cherished as long as any who knew him remain. He was a giant in our time, endowed with many talents, each of which he used to the full. Surely his greatest gift was his generous nature from which he dealt in lavish portions to all who crossed his path, and it was this generosity of nature, so evident in his care and concern for people, that made him admired and loved by so many. He once remarked, "If only people would realize how much of religion consists in merely being kind."

How natural was the phone call, a note of appreciation, or a visit! His visitations and public appearances did not lessen with the years, even when his ministry broadened after retirement. In all kinds of weather he would turn up at gatherings and functions. Sickness and bereavement found him present, and his hosting of friends and visitors continued unabated.

He was a big man, five feet eleven inches tall and of large frame. As he walked in procession attired in episcopal robes he made a striking figure, towering over all. His character depended on his deep and firm faith in the providence of a loving God. It seemed always to be the guiding force in his life, as a young man, as a soldier, in his pastoral ministry, and in his personal grief on the death of his wife. Not by preaching or writing but in the way he lived, he drew people to him and then through him to a religious view of life. In him the practicality of the gospel was made plain for all to see.

At the time of his death an editorial appeared in *The Toronto Sun* entitled "God's Gallant Warrior." It described the bishop's life and accomplishments, and compared him to some of the world's heros. "It is among this courageous company that Frederick Hugh Wilkinson can be counted. To paraphrase Shakespeare: 'He was man, take him for all in all, we shall not look upon his like again.' And he was God's man besides."

How fitting that on his last night on earth he should host a dinner party at the Toronto Hunt Club. Afterward he walked to his car, and there death came to him like an old friend for whom he had long prepared.

> So he passed over, and all the trumpets sounded for
> him on the other side.
>
> *John Bunyan*

THE EARLY YEARS

On Canada's southeastern coast in the Province of Nova Scotia lies the capital city and port of Halifax. The city is on a hill that slopes down to Chebucto Bay, known as Halifax Harbor. It was to Halifax that thousands of American colonists arrived during the War of Independence to settle and ultimately to be known as United Empire Loyalists. It was here again, during the War of 1812 between Britain and the United States, that privateers used the port as a base of operations. During the American Civil War it was a haven for Confederate blockade runners, and of course during World War II it was the base of operations for the great convoys. The outer harbor has berths for ocean liners and huge modern freighters, and the inner harbor, because of its size and depth, can accommodate the world's combined navies.

On the northeast side of the harbour lies Dartmouth, which is connected to Halifax by two modern bridges but at the time of this story was entirely dependent upon transportation by ferry. To Dartmouth in the spring of 1894, to minister to its people, arrived the Reverend Fred Wilkinson accompanied by his wife Jenny and their year old son Harold. The new rector of Christ Church was a strong resourceful character and an enthusiast of the evangelical wing of the Church of England. He provided leadership for a growing congregation. His experience in the business world, prior to his entrance into the ministry, gave him a unique administrative ability which was to stand him in good stead in his new vocation. He was an avid gardener and planted some forty individual gardens over the next few years, to the delight of all the citizens of Dartmouth. He also set himself to work making superb maps of the journeys of St Paul, which he hung in his study and other places; his children remembered those maps for many years.

Within a year of his arrival the new rector had installed electric lighting in the church, somewhat earlier than the churches nearby. He formed the various women's organizations of the parish into a guild and began a visitation of the entire area. In 1896 the free pew system was adopted. He must have been a strong advocate for this because, when he went to Toronto some years later, it was the first item on the agenda of his first vestry meeting. In 1898 a stained glass window depicting the ascension was installed in the chancel, a drive was started to erect a Sunday school building, and a program of renovation and refurbishing the church including new seats was undertaken.

The year 1896 is of great importance to this story, for early on the morning of 18 November, Frederick Hugh Wilkinson was born in the rectory of Christ Church. Within six weeks, on 3 January 1897, he was baptised by the Reverend Dyson Hague, the famous Prayer Book scholar and the rector of St Paul's Church in Halifax. To the Wilkinsons were born three sons Harold, Fred, and Heber; and two daughters Jean and later Ruth. The latter was born after the family had arrived in Toronto.

The Wilkinson family lived in Dartmouth for ten years, and Fred for eight of these; so he spent his formative years in sight and call of the sea. And what a call it must have been to a boy in his most impressionable years, watching the ships of the Royal Navy anchor in the harbour prepared for them by Captain James Cook, the great navigator and explorer. Each spring the British North American Squadron arrived at their summer station in Halifax and on certain occasions would parade to Christ Church for divine service to the playing of "Hearts of Oak," the grand sea tune of the Royal Navy. During this period British troops garrisoned Halifax as one of its major outposts, and the atmosphere bristled with empire, discipline, and duty. In later years one of Fred's most vivid memories would be the changing the guard on Citadel Hill.

The children of the family described Dartmouth as very much like an English village, and the inhabitants lived as villagers do, a close community gathered around the church. There were many picnics to McNabs Island by rowboat, and bathing in Cow Bay with its large sandy beach. Greenvale was a school where all ages attended — common in those days — and here at the age of six young Fred commenced what was to be a long period of schooling. He was an average student and tended to have a short attention span. Once, when his father asked why he was late from school, Fred said he had been put in the closet. Immediately his father marched to the school and demanded to know why Fred had suffered such treatment. The teacher Miss Hamilton replied, "Because he was daydreaming." When his father cautioned her never to put any child in the closet for any reason, she responded, "He'll either be a dreamer or a great man some day." While her method may be questionable, her assessment proved to be prophetic.

At dinner one evening in November of 1904 the Reverend Fred Wilkinson announced to his family that on 1 December they were leaving Dartmouth to live in Toronto. On the eve of his eighth birthday Frederick Hugh faced the first of many leave takings. The young seem to weather the change of uprooting better than most. New friends appear; the home, the school, the city are quickly accepted. This is the natural progression of youth. Yet those eight years in Dartmouth made their lasting impression on Frederick Hugh. His love of the sea and respect for things British were often displayed in his writings and addresses, the last of these in the year before his death.

It was in the final days of 1904 that the Wilkinson family, now six in number, arrived in the city that was to play a most important part in their lives. Toronto at this time boasted a population of a quarter of a million, and was by any standard a large and flourishing city. The annexation of Parkdale, Yorkville, and a host of other small suburbs had increased its size, but the greatest growth came from immigration, which was wide open in all North America. Passage from Europe to America was at one stage as low as $10.00! While most Europeans headed for the American cities, the British came to Canada and in the main to Toronto, where in 1914 86 per cent of the population was of British origin.

At the turn of the century the city was very much in the Victorian age. There was a smug righteous air about it that infuriated its neighbours. To the rest of Canada it was known as hog town, and visitors and tourists alike painted it in the gloomiest terms. On Sunday everything was closed except churches, of which there were more than in any other city of America. Torontonians prided themselves on being "the city of churches." Only after bitter debate was the street railway system allowed to operate on the sabbath, provided the tram cars stopped at every church on their route. Despite this, or perhaps because of it, Toronto was a good city to live in. Its crime rate was the lowest on the continent, its sanitation and public health were far ahead of other large municipalities, its fire fighting service was the pride of the city, and Canada's two largest department stores dominated its downtown core.

It was known internationally for its leaders in the world of sports: men such as Tom Longboat, one of the fastest runners of all time, who won the Boston marathon in 1907 setting a record for 25 miles in just 2 hours. In 1904 Lou Scholes was the first of several Canadians to win the diamond sculls in rowing at Henley in England. Joe Wright, Sr, from the Toronto

Argonaut rowing club competed five times over the course at Henley and won both the British and USA sculls, as did his son, Joe Wright, Jr. Ned Hanlon was the idol of Toronto for his legendary rowing which saw him take the championships of Canada, the United States, and finally the world. Hollywood and Broadway hosted a large colony of Canadians including Mary Pickford, "America's sweetheart," and Beatrice Lillie, the "toast of London" and longest reigning star on the world stage. Garfield Weston left a Toronto bakery to head one of the world's largest merchandising empires in London, England, a feat to be duplicated in the press world by Roy Thomson, another Torontonian.

Needless to say the churches formed the centre of activity for most of the city. Plays, concerts, and meetings of all kinds took place in church buildings. On Sunday hundreds attended morning and evening services, and afternoon Bible classes and Sunday school. To this city, and to an active religious and community life at St Peter's Church on Carlton Street, came the Wilkinson family of three boys and one girl, shortly to be joined by Ruth, their last child.

The new Rector quickly made his presence felt among the people of St Peter's. At his first vestry meeting he presented a proposal for free seats; after much debate this was adopted. Anxious to upgrade the music, he did a daring thing for those days, and brought Mr Gurney from Harrow in England to be organist and choirmaster. Later Mr Hutchins was brought also from England to replace him. Although Mr Wilkinson was not musical himself, he appreciated the value of music and made each of his children take music lessons. All who knew him agreed that he was a strong authoritative figure. He was a strict disciplinarian though a loving one, as his daughter Jean is quick to point out. He would not allow the children to quarrel. "Jean, you love your brother, don't you!" he would demand, and she would reluctantly agree. Mrs Wilkinson was a beautiful woman with a disposition to match. Neighbours and parishoners thought highly of her, and admired the loving care and concern she showed for all. In the manner of those days she deferred to her husband's judgment, yet they discussed things together, and it was understood that decisions were mutually agreed upon.

The children were encouraged to think independently and were allowed to have their own magazines. Duty was an important word in the family. Jean and Ruth agree on the importance of their parents' discipline. "We would never think of correcting or arguing with them. I guess it never did any harm to us. We knew we were very important to them." Or again, "Father and Mother set standards we wouldn't dream of breaking," says Jean. "No swearing was high on the list. I remember Heber being very cross and upset about something and emitting some very ill-chosen words. Father emerged from his study and put Heber across his knee. Bang, Bang: 'We don't talk that way my son'."

All the children loved sports. Tennis, swimming, and hockey played an important part in their growing up. There were two tennis courts on the grounds of the church, for use by members, and in winter an excellent rink for hockey. "I would stand on the edge of the bathtub," says Ruth, "and look longingly out of the window at my brothers who were allowed to play after dinner." Every day began with family morning prayer and then school. The girls were sent to Havergal, a girls private school on Jarvis Street, now the home of the Canadian Broadcasting Company, and the boys, dressed in short pants and Eton jacket with wide white collar, to the model school at Gerrard and Church Street, later to become the normal school and now the site of Ryerson College. On Mondays Tommy Church would call for Mr Wilkinson, and the two would walk to the normal school where the one taught religious knowledge, the other "civics." Tommy Church later would become seven-time mayor of the city and a great favourite with the soldiers during the war.

Of his later gift of communication, Frederick Hugh showed no early promise. Immediately after his first public appearance at a Christmas concert, having recited his allotted three lines, he ran home and was ill. There were no such qualms, however, about his greatest love. He was a born musician. Early in Halifax days the Nordheimer piano that is still in the family possession was purchased for the musical education of the children. We have no record of Fred's teacher there, but in Toronto he studied with a Miss Darby on Carlton Street, and with the two English organists in residence at St Peters. He practiced without urging or coaxing. "None of the family seemed to mind being wakened at six AM when Fred was practicing," says his sister Ruth. He played the piano regularly for the Sunday school, and at 8:30 AM every day he played for chapel at Havergal girls school and then ran all the way to Jarvis Collegiate. He was still in short pants at the time, and his sister Jean, who was one of the pupils at Havergal says, "Did it ever embarrass me to have my brother do this." In later years Fred told me that he somehow managed to successfully conceal from his pals at school why he was late every morning.

Fred next went as a student to Mr Whealdon, the musical director at Metropolitan Church, the cathedral of Methodism in Toronto. His association with Whealdon was a rich and rewarding one which he would refer to often in later years. By now an accomplished organist, he played on occasion for the Sunday service on the great organ, the gift of the Massey family. Occasionally he would play for his teacher on the organ in the home of Lillian Massey on Jarvis Street. Few people who knew him later in life, in his pastoral capacity, were aware that he was other than a talented amateur musician. His sister Jean says, "Music was Fred's predominating friend all through his life at every stage." He excelled not only in his understanding and appreciation of music, but in the performance of it. His was not merely technical performance, but a complete experience in which he was lost to all around him.

I will always remember the time toward the end of his life when he asked me if I would like him to play for me. I replied that I would like to hear Mozart; so he sat down and played a

number of Mozart sonatas. It was a rich moment, and it led us
to ponder the possibility of a career on the concert stage, which
is what he could have had, and what he wanted, until other
factors intervened. As we trace his life, it will be seen again and
again how music enters in and plays a significant part. He had
given piano recitals at an early age, and on the last morning of
his life he rehearsed at some length for a coming recital in St
Paul's Church.

It was not possible to perceive the bishop's artistry on sight.
Of ruddy complexion, dark hair, and robust frame he
appeared as an athlete, trained and ready for the fray. But this
exterior impression was softened by an irrepressible sense of
humour, which was to stand him in good stead all his life. He is
remembered as a "laughing, happy boy." Friends recall the
handsome family in the second pew of St Peters, the two girls
Jean and Ruth on one side of the mother, the three boys
Harold, Fred, and Heber on the other. Mrs Eleaner James
remembers how some of the Havergal girls would attend services on Sunday morning, sitting on the transept across from
the Wilkinson pew. She writes, "Mysteriously we never seemed to have service books, and Fred or Heber would bring them
to us; you can picture the excitement in our young teenage
lives." Heber in later years married one of the girls, Rowena
Stringer.

Fred had the happiest of memories of growing up in Toronto. He learned to swim at the YMCA, although he had been
taught some of the rudiments in the Atlantic waters off
Halifax. There is no record of his having tested the waters of
the Don or Humber Rivers, although both of these were clean
then and in much use, as were the beaches of Lake Ontario.
Riverdale Park and Allan Gardens were both within a short
walking distance and very popular. The former had a zoo, and
band concerts regularly took place in both parks. On Sundays
ladies in their long dresses and men impeccably turned out
strolled through the grounds viewing the flowers and listening
to the music. The district was one of affluence. Carlton, Sher-

bourne, and Jarvis Streets were the setting for large stately homes fronted by beautiful gardens, all maintained by domestic staff. The well known racing family of Abe Orpen lived at the corner of Sherbourne and Carlton Streets. The son Fred Orpen was a great friend of Fred Wilkinson, whose boyhood chums included Arthur Smoke, later a prominent lawyer, and Cuthbert Robinson who was to become the Bishop of Moosonee. On Jarvis Street lived Chester Massey whose son Raymond was to become the famous actor; the other son Vincent became governor general of Canada. On the same street lived Walter Massey whose only son Denton was to make his name known in church and state as founder and leader of the world's largest Bible class, and member for Toronto-Greenwood with the largest plurality in the House of Commons. Canon Cody, later to be president and then chancellor of the University of Toronto, lived here as did the Gooderhams of whisky fame.

Chief justice Sir William Mulock lived on Jarvis Street, and it was his grandson William, later to become postmaster general, who was Fred's greatest friend. Another was Allen Peuchen. His father Major Peuchan had survived the sinking of the Titanic. Peuchen, a vice-commodore of the Royal Canadian Yacht Club, had identified himself as such to the ship's personnel and was assisting in launching lifeboats. Number Six boat was being lowered when it was discovered it contained only one seaman. Second Officer Lightoller, motioning to a rope hanging from the davit above, asked Peuchan to go down and assist in Number Six. The rope was some ten feet away from the side of the ship, but Peuchan made it. Also in Number Six was the famous Molly Brown. Peuchan took three oranges from his cabin leaving $300,000 in stocks and bonds on the table.

Senator David Walker has vivid memories of life in those days. He was a member of St Peters and sang in the boy's choir. He recalls, "Fred was quite a hero to me. The first time I saw him he and 'Tut' Swan were fighting. It was a knock-down drag-out fight, really bitter, knocking over chairs and tables; they were very angry with each other. Later they were great friends." The Senator goes on to say, "Fred had some of the fireworks of the father, unlike his brother Harold who was more like the mother. Fred was going to be a professional musician and was quite an authority on music. He would go all over to hear musicians in recital. He had a bright career ahead of him."

In an attempt to arrive at a decision about his vocation, Harold left university after his first year to take a job on the lines of the Northern Electric Company. Fred and Harold were very close, and there is no doubt that Harold's decision to work helped Fred to decide to do the same. In his turn he also went into the business world, taking a job as clerk with the Confederation Life Insurance Company, where he was to remain for some two years. It would be more correct to say he stuck it out for two years; his immediate superior was a very disagreeable sort who went out of his way to make things rough for the new boy.

The year is 1913 and the time of Fred's graduation from Jarvis Collegiate. On Bloor Street near Jarvis the new St Paul's Anglican Church is being built. A magnificent edifice, it was to have a splendid organ, and Fred spent much of his time here in the summer of 1913, eager to assist and learn during the installation of the instrument. He was the first student to play this organ, and it was here that he commenced a lifelong friendship with Healy Willan, the great organist and composer. He would later say, "I never thought that I would one day return to St Paul's as its Rector." Later in the year Fred reported for work at Confederation Life. Two sons of the rectory now toiled in the business world, the third, Heber, would in time follow suit.

It is often the case in a disciplined household that the parents urge their children in one direction or another; such was not the case in the Wilkinson family. The father, as we have seen, was a strict disciplinarian; he had high Christian standards which he lived up to and which he expected others to abide by. He brought his children up in this way, and they loyally conformed. About their vocation he would advise and guide, but he never tried to push the children into anything, particularly his sons into the ministry. In Fred's case he did question the financial benefits to be had from music, but it was a logical view and one that any father would have taken, particularly in those days. Cecil Swanson, then student curate to the rector, writes of him, "I got along well with him, and when I went to the Yukon he paid my salary there. They were a good family, all caring for each other, and there was a fine mutual love between them." Senator Walker says, "He threw me out of the choir for misbehaving. He was strict but kindly. He got along well with Fred, thought the world of him and, of course, of all of his children." Fred often spoke in later years of their happy loving home life and the influence it had on him in later years.

In connection with home life I once discussed with the bishop the work of Havelock Ellis, published under the titled *A Study In British Genius.* In this study, which has become a classic, Ellis found that, of the outstanding leaders in the British empire, by far the largest number were sons and daughters of the clergy. They outnumbered all of the other professions combined and had seven times greater chance of turning out exceptionally well than any other child. Vishner of the University of Chicago carried out the study in the United States with exactly the same results. Of the signers of the Declaration of Independence, nine were the sons of clergymen and ten out of fifty-one were in the Hall of Fame. Both studies attribute the success of the children to a good home life: not affluence, for the clergy had none of this; not academic opportunity, for the children of other professions had more opportunity of education; but a home in which spiritual and moral discipline formed an important part of the family life. "Here, here, cried Fred," as he reminisced on his own life. Then in that deep voice of his he said, "Nothing is of greater importance than what is taught and caught in the home."

As the year drew to a close hydro power from Niagara Falls was brought to Toronto amid gala festivities to mark the event. Electric lighting appeared on downtown streets. On Davenport Hill the family of Sir Henry Pellat moved into Casa Loma, which was to become widely known through Glen Gray and his Casa Loma orchestra. Everyone in the city went to see the magnificent castle. Fred, now gainfully employed, could afford to take in concerts and recitals at Massey Hall and other places. Senator Walker remembers, "On Sunday afternoons my mother, who was an accomplished pianist, would have musical soirées, and on occasion Harold, Fred, and Joe McCulley would be present. We would all go to church afterward; everybody went to church in those days."

Life seemed simple and uncomplicated, entertainment was self-made and took place in people's homes. Discussion groups, parlour games, and singsongs were the order of the day at every gathering. Every church had large Bible classes, and scouting played a tremendous part in the life of the community. There were missionary nights at all churches, when the young people collected and made up barrels and boxes of things to be sent to Indian missions, the Eskimos, and missionaries on duty in Africa and other places. There was a high sense of idealism on the part of these young men and women, higher than ever before and perhaps since. Steeped in religious precepts they could hardly fail to be otherwise. It was a wonderful time to be young; it was the best of times, all too soon to end so tragically for so many. "The old world in its sunset was fair to see," said Churchill. In 1913 a new song called "Tipperary" was written by an English music hall comedian and was soon to be on the lips of millions. It was the last year of peace for a world that would never be the same again. There was little or no indication, even in the highest circles, of the carnage that lay ahead. With seeming prescience the hymn writer Baring Gould had written, "Crowns and thrones may perish, Kingdoms rise and wane," and with them the flower of Europe's youth was to disappear from the world.

IN FLANDERS FIELDS

1914 will be remembered as one of the saddest years of history. On 28 June 1914 the heir to the Austrian throne and his wife were assassinated during a state visit to Serbia. Almost a month passed and it seemed that the issue had been forgotten, but behind the scenes the warmongers were hard at work. Assassination was not a new thing; only months earlier King George of Greece had been similarly dispatched, and in 1903 the king of Serbia, the queen and her two brothers, were killed in the Royal Palace. There is evidence in the latter case that both Russia and Austria-Hungary knew of the murder and may have instigated it.

The assassination of the archduke, however, was an opportunity to settle innumerable old scores. The second Balkan War had ended in 1913 to the satisfaction of none of the participants. The rivalries, jealousies, and suspicions remained, the flames being fanned by the larger powers. Quietly Austrian diplomats drew up an ultimatum to Serbia in which they were supported by German diplomats and by the German general staff; it was presented to Serbia on 23 July. It was an incredible document, deliberately designed for impossible acceptance. Although Serbia accepted nearly all of the terms, Austria Hungary declared war against her on 28 July. Now, as mobilization began in Germany, Russia, and France, the many peace lovers tried to avert calamity. The Austrian emperor, both old and sick, did not want war; the Czar tried to pass the dispute on to the International Court at the Hague; the Kaiser, on a three week cruise, did not realize until his hurried return the extent to which his ministers had aggravated the situation. Letters were exchanged; cables were sent in an attempt to reach a settlement. But there was no stopping the evil unleashed by hate, and a desire on the part of some for a place in history. On 4 August France and Belgium were invaded, and Britain entered a war that was to embroil much of the world for over four years. Poison gas and trench warfare were introduced. Vast armies lived opposite each other in the most horrible conditions, emerging periodically to slaughter enormous numbers of men for a few feet of mud. The casualties were appalling: eight and a half million dead, over twenty-one million wounded, and seven-and-a-half million made prisoner or missing. The war brought about the fall of the dynasties of Europe, opened the door to communism, and sowed the seeds of World War II.

As Europe blissfully drifted toward war, the new world remained equally ignorant of the cataclysm about to burst upon it. After an initial notice of the assassination of the archduke, the *Toronto Globe* reported a brief account of the funeral on 3 July. During the next three weeks the paper reported the death and funeral of Joseph Chamberlain the English statesman, the Henley Regatta which Canada lost, the Canadian rifle team at Bisley, the damage to crops in the West because of the drought, assorted Canadian and American news, and results of the home rule debate in London. Then on 25 July there appeared in a lead column the Austrian ultimatum; yet all who remember the first account admit they never dreamed that in nine days the British Empire would be engaged in a terrible war in which Canada would be heavily committed.

In 1939 war was greeted with solemn and grim determination in all countries on both sides; not so in 1914. In St Petersburg, Vienna, Berlin, Paris, and London, patriotic fervour amounting to mass hysteria was the order of the day.

Everyone believed it was to be a short war, and the rush was on to be at the finish. In Toronto the news was greeted with flags, bands, and large crowds of singing, cheering people. Men flocked to the armories to enlist, and within two months the first Canadian contingent was ready to sail for England. With it were three battalions from Toronto. Hardly a home remained unaffected, and from the rectory on Carlton Street in December of that year Harold Wilkinson enlisted.

He was a scholarship student and was about to return to university when war broke out. An active scout leader and a teacher of a large class of boys in Sunday school, he had an instinct for loving service, and there seemed no doubt that he had made the decision to enter the ministry. Miss E.M. Knox, a family friend and a great admirer of Fred and Harold, in a published article in 1917, tells of an evening they spent together when Harold's future was under discussion. She says she was utterly convinced he had already dedicated his life to the ministry. Of quiet gentle disposition, not easily swayed or influenced by propaganda, he seemed the least likely fellow to enlist in the Eaton Machine Gun battalion or even to handle a gun. In an upper room in the rectory where he and Fred studied, they talked of the war and, naturally, whether or not Fred should enlist. Harold was totally opposed to the idea. He very much wanted Fred to pursue his music; this was a great gift and must be put to work. Fred must also take his place as the elder brother at home and try to fill the gap made by his absence. Finally Fred was to take over his Sunday school class, the importance of which he expressed in these words: "There is no greater work than looking after these boys."

At the exhibition grounds enlistees arrived from recruitment centres for their initial training and outfitting. There were delays while the factories geared up to produce uniforms and guns, and in addition learned to cope with an outbreak of meningitis. Among its first victims Harold was stricken with a particularly virulent form and hovered near death for many days. Dick Meech, the butcher's son who had often delivered meat to the Wilkinson home and had played baseball with Harold, by chance occupied the stall next to him in the exhibition pig pens. He can remember Harold terribly delirious and finally being moved to the Toronto General Hospital. Many had already died, and it wasn't expected that Harold would live.

"Time came for the battalion to leave, and the commanding officer announced we were not going overseas without saying goodbye to one of our comrades; so we paraded to the hospital. Harold was wheeled out onto a balcony, and we cheered lustily. Then, smartly lining up, we gave him a formal salute. He waved back." For weeks he remained in hospital, but after three more weeks of convalescence at home he left for overseas to rejoin his unit, reaching them in France during May 1915 in time to take part in the second battle of Ypres. It was in the Ypres salient that Canadians were first engaged in combat in the early spring of 1915, and the Germans launched the first gas attack on 22 April. There is no record of Harold's reaction to the misery of trench warfare in which he fought for more than a year, but there are some accounts of his next posting which was to the Royal Flying Corps in October 1916.

As the first full year of the war drew to a close it was beginning to dawn on all that the conflict was spreading in scope as well as intensity. The names of the casualties appeared daily in the press, bringing home to Canadians the stark reality of Flanders Fields. In 1915 the Germans proclaimed a blockade of Britain, and bombed London and the ports from airships called Zepplins. They executed nurse Edith Cavel in Belgium and sank over one million tons of merchant shipping, including the passenger liner *Lusitania.* The year brought Italy into the war and saw the landings in Gallipoli of British troops and their withdrawal in December in what was to be termed a devastating defeat. In Toronto men were still enlisting, women were signing up as nurses and volunteers, and everyone was knitting clothing for "boys at the front." Dazzling recruiting posters appeared everywhere, and rallies gathered in front of the City Hall attended by bands and featuring prominent speakers, but the glamour of war had died with the repeated arrival of casualty lists.

Fred was now in residence at Wycliffe College on the campus of the University of Toronto. He had left Confederation Life in the fall and enrolled in Arts, majoring in orientals and music; his stint in the business world had made him more determined than ever to pursue music as a career. He played the organ for chapel in the College and gave several recitals on the great organ in Convocation Hall. He played squash and was active on the swim team and hockey team. Study came easily to him now; he passed all subjects with good marks at the end of his first term. He went home to spend the Christmas holidays at the rectory; it was to be the last happy Christmas for some years. At a watchnight service the family solemnly welcomed 1916. It was on this occasion that Fred resolved what he must do; within a few days he disclosed to his parents his intention to enlist. They naturally did their best to dissuade him, pointing out that he had just turned nineteen and surely ought to wait a little longer; but he countered by saying how difficult it was to stand by and see his friends answering the call to duty, and his classmates almost daily disappearing from school. He felt in good conscience that he could no longer postpone what he knew was inevitable. On 6 January 1916 he reported for his medical at the University Armories and was sworn to active service on 1 February. He weighed in at 133 pounds, stood 5' 9½" and was nineteen years, two months of age. Because he had some militia training in the Second Field Company of the Canadian Engineers, he chose the engineers on enlisting and was assigned to the Third Division Signal Company.

From Exhibition Park he went to Lansdowne Park in Ottawa. One of his first tasks was to clean down the horses that formed part of the Third Divisional Force. His description of this task was amusing: knowing nothing about horses he sallied into the stall with comb and brush to be met with a hefty kick in the groin which sent him across the stable. As he put it:

"I almost ended my career then and there." From the outset he enjoyed every minute of military service. All his life he evinced concern and care for people, and this never showed to better advantage than during the war. He was always happy, laughing, and eager to be a friend. Consequently he made many friends, quickly and firmly; all of whom remember Fred "as a young gentleman of great character." One fine spring evening he and his comrades sailed on the SS Metagami, arriving in England on 25 March 1916 and continuing on to Bramshot for advanced training.

Bert Diltz writes, "At Bramshot in the spring of 1916 a dark-complexioned, rosy-cheeked youth, who appeared never overweight but always outgrowing his uniform, formed fours with the rest in the brown dust of the parade ground. His eyes were dark and deep and his countenance contemplative. He was neither aloof nor indulgent, but kept his thoughts to himself. Since he talked little and listened attentively, no one knew much about him. Every night and morning in a hut occupied by thirty-five others, he got down on his knees beside his three soft pine boards and two blankets to say his prayers. This practice occasionally brought forth some rude comments but never a retort in kind, not even a smile of compassion. Self-righteousness was not in his nature. Once the unit got to France, however, all comments ceased and the quite reflective youth soon became accepted affectionately as Wilkie." On 5 June 1916 he was transferred to the Fourth Division Signal Company as a "sapper" and dispatched to France on 11 August. The term "sapper" denotes one who erects breastworks and fortifications as well as anything to do with these. Fred was specifically a "linesman." It was his job to lay communication lines between battalion, brigade, and divisional headquarters, as well as to maintain them — which was a heavy job as they were constantly being broken.

It has been said that he liked being a linesman because it kept him outdoors in the fresh air where freedom of action was still available. He also told me, "I am glad that I never had to take a life." So if he had a choice of unit to join (and this is questionable), from all accounts he would probably have chosen signals. All soldiers were instructed in small arms, and linesmen were required to carry a rifle and 60 rounds of ammunition when repairing lines. When laying new lines the linesmen were provided with a team of horses and a wagon to carry equipment, but for most of the work they had to travel to trouble spots on foot. In emergency a runner would carry a message, but in one instance during the battle of the Somme, Fred rode into brigade headquarters on a horse, to the delight of his friend Bert Diltz who hadn't seen him since leaving England. Compared to the stagnancy of trench warfare, lineswork involved constant movement and change of pace; but it was a dangerous role, for the enemy was well aware of the advantages of broken communications and was constantly on the lookout for the linesmen searching for broken lines. The loose ends, often blown some feet apart, would have to be located, stripped, joined together, and taped, often in view of the enemy and exposed to their fire.

The battle of the Somme raged from 1 July to 13 November 1916, and the British losses alone amounted to over four hundred and twenty thousand. During this period "Wilkie was indefatigable," says Diltz. "He could go without food and rest for long periods, always never too weary to go the extra sacrificial mile without a murmur. The mud and misery between Posieres and Courcelette were as familiar to him as the cold and drenching rains which fell continually from leaden skies. He accepted his lot as the assignment of fate, a duty to be perfomed without question or hesitation." An avid reader, he carried two volumes of Sir Walter Scott in his napsack. His father regularly sent him reading material which he would pass on to Diltz who would give him things to read in return. Whenever off duty he occupied himself in reading, walking, and talking with whomever he could find. He would often hitch a ride to attend divine service or explore some town or city. "Friendly and sociable he nevertheless had abundant resources to entertain himself," writes Diltz. "Surrounded by companions with whom he had spiritually little in common, he was always courteous and considerate. He never used a bad word although many others did."

Harry Tonkin who was with him for over two years says, "I liked Wilkie; we got along very well. No matter where you saw him he was always the same, very friendly. He had a tough time over there, all the cussing and swearing, but he took it in good part. Some of us tried to restrain our language when he was around."

Diltz adds, "In times of great urgency the flame of his resolution burned with a steady glow; in times of distress when the incongruity of the sergeant's cursing seemed to lighten the task, Wilkie perceived the humour of the situation and laughed as heartily as anyone else." Many of these men confessed to the influence Fred made on them, but they also made their mark on him for the rest of his life. He marvelled at their courage and at the way in which they adapted to the most trying circumstances. He told me about one incident. When he was making his way through a crossroads, a voice shouted, "Wilkie." On turning he saw a pal of his seated on the back of a gun carriage cheerily waving to him, and on drawing nearer it became obvious the man had been reading. Fred said, "Shelling was taking place; the area was a sea of mud, dashing cavalry, gun carriages, and ambulances; and here sat this fellow reading *The Meditations of Marcus Aurelius*." Most of all he would remember the camaraderie that only such a conflict could engender, and a comradeship greater than those men had known before or since. He had a great inner strength which permitted him to look beyond that which was seen, and he was quick to sense this in others. It was this period in his life that accounts for the sense of mysticism in his writing and speaking in later years.

There is no record of Fred's letters from overseas, and it is probable that he destroyed them himself. Through the writings of Miss Knox, however, we do have a glimpse of

Harold's letters describing his experience in some cathedral town or the hospitality extended to him in some country house. He tells of the courage of the chaps he is with and reflects upon his own circumstances. "God has given me my life many times; and if he sees fit to bring me back, after this horrible conflict, to my dear ones and friends, I have realized that my life can only be devoted to serving him in whatever work he wishes me to do." He is pleased when he comes out second in a race, "Not bad for a non-smoker," and he remembers Heber, his younger brother at home, burning with impatience to be with him, and tells him that the good work he is doing "counts for as much as we are doing over here." He ponders in his letters whether he may be flying over Fred and longs that some dive may bring him into his company, an event that did occur although not through a dive. Bert Diltz remembers distinctly the day Fred introduced him to a young man in officer's uniform of the Royal Flying Corps. Harold was as fair as Fred was dark. Diltz says, "He, too, was the reflective type with no delusions about the aims and purposes of the war." Yet he, like Fred, was completely dedicated to the cause at hand. He invented a new scheme of signalling and an improvement in aerial photography. Too soon they parted, Harold to his squadron and Fred to the trenches.

It was March 1917. Revolution had broken out in Russia, and mutiny was widespread among the French troups. It fell to the British to open the spring offensive which began at Vimy Ridge. Coming out of the lines after a long tour of duty Wilkie and some others, bone weary, trooped to a dugout, threw themselves on the ground, and went to sleep. An officer came in and asked for two volunteers to repair the lines; Wilkie and Harry Tonkin stood up and went out. The place was just east of Cobourg Tunnel and below where the Vimy memorial now stands. The date was 17 March, the night the British released the famous unsuccessful gas attack from the top of the ridge. The counter-attack was devastating. Tonkin says, "We had to maintain the line up to brigade; they were shelling the heck out

of us. As soon as we would fix it, they would break it again."
They worked through fire and fatigue until relieved the following day. For action during this period Fred was awarded the
Military Medal. The official citation reads, "For continuous
good work night and day through this period [five days] on the
maintenance of lines. He went out voluntarily on several occasions to repair lines under heavy shell fire. His absolute
disregard of danger and coolness under very trying conditions
were a very large factor in the maintenance of communications
across this area." Tonkin was deservedly to receive the
Military Medal for later action.

Vimy Ridge was captured by the Canadians on 10 April. At
Souchez Valley, just behind the ridge, Wilkie and Tonkin were
again sent out to find the broken lines. There were shell holes
everywhere; it had snowed during the night. Tonkin says, "We
found the line, but I stepped through the ice and sank up to my
neck. I shouted to Wilkie, "Don't come over here," but he came
anyway and fell in also. We found the line, repaired it, and
reported back to the officer and signal office. We then went
into a dugout, and Wilkie took off all his clothes and wrapped
himself in a blanket. I stripped down to my underwear,
wrapped myself in a blanket, and we went to sleep. In the
morning his underwear was frozen, which he donned under his
uniform and went out."

It was some time before Fred learned Harold had been shot
down in May and was now in hospital in England. It was a
head wound and serious, yet it seemed that after many weeks
he would pull through. Mrs Alan Peuchen of Toronto was a
volunteer at Queen Alexandra Hospital where Harold was a
patient. She kept the family informed of his condition, which
soon improved so much that plans were made for him to return
home to convalesce. But in early September his health began to
deteriorate, and Fred was given special leave to visit. For five
days the two were together as much as Harold's condition
would permit. The talk was of loved ones and their future
plans, Harold saying that if spared he would enter the

ministry. Many years later, with a quiet voice and a faraway look in his eyes, Fred spoke to me of that last time with Harold. At Harold's request, a piano was moved into the room and Fred played for him. I suspect that the music of Beethoven and Mozart, which they both loved, would certainly have been included, but I am sure that Fred would also have played Harold's favorite hymn, "Jesus, Saviour, pilot me."

All too quickly the leave ended and with a parting embrace Fred said farewell to his brother for the last time. Within a few days of his departure for France, Harold died. The body was shipped to Toronto for a full military funeral on 20 October 1917. Senator Walker says, "Harold's funeral was one of the most impressive Toronto had ever seen." Of all the influences on Fred's life nothing was to have a greater impact than the death of Harold. It is common to extol the virtues of one taken early in life, to say, "He was the flower of the family." But it was much more than this with Fred; Harold was always his shining star. He was familiar of course with the words of McRae's poem "In Flanders Fields" published in 1915: "To you from failing hands we throw the torch, be yours to hold it high." Quietly he vowed to fill the place made vacant by Harold's death. Although a dedicated Christian, Fred had intended to pursue a career in music and not in the church. Senator Walker says, "He told me it was Harold's death that made him decide to give up music as a career and to go into the ministry." This statement is borne out by others. Walker goes on to say, "Up to that time I don't think he had any intention of going into the church; he wasn't the type to enter the ministry. He was quite a boy, not scrappy but a real he-man, a great fellow in every way."

In the year of conflict left to him he had ample opportunity to consider the shortness and uncertainty of life. After his return from leave in September he was continually involved in the third battle of Ypres. Week after week a series of encounters took place in which small portions of ground were exchanged for large losses of human life.

Passchendaele was the ultimate in unbelievable horror. The area was a vast sea of mud where men repeatedly slipped and fell and often waded knee deep. To fall into a shell hole was a common and devastating experience; they were full of filthy water and contaminated by death and gas; the victim had to be pulled out by a comrade's extended rifle. To this was added the interminable rain and the pounding from German artillery. The place was taken by the British on 4 November in what has been described as an empty victory. Not one building remained standing in the town which had been won at terrible cost in dead, missing, and wounded. From the shambles of this carnage, which Lloyd George referred to as "the battle of the mud," Fred emerged a hero. Diltz writes: "Wilkie spent seven days with little relief and caked with mud from the waist down. Medicinal rum was the only source of warmth available, but Wilkie refused his issue, saying that since he had come thus far without it, he was prepared to go on to the end. Seen in retrospect, such a decision appears too profound for human understanding to fathom. At any rate it was here that Wilkie first revealed the signs of utter physical fatigue in a most unusual way. His solicitude for a shell-shocked companion appeared feeble and fumbling. The burdens the human spirit can sustain never cease to be amazing, with or without rum, and the war for an imaginative youth, could be a suffocating weight."

It was at Passchendaele that a companion while repairing lines had his leg blown off. Fred took off his belt, wrapped it around the poor fellow's stump, carried him to the bearers and then on to the casualty station. Fred told me, "I thought when they took him away it was the end of him; but years later when I was speaking in Calgary a fellow came up to me and tapping his leg with a cane said, 'Wilkie you saved my life.' What a thrill it was seeing that man again; it was my one happy association with Passchendaele." The year was to end with the battle of Cambrai, made famous by the use of tanks on a large

The Rev and Mrs Fred Wilkinson, parents of the bishop.

Frederick Hugh, five years old.

Frederick Hugh at the organ in Convocation Hall, University of Toronto.

"Wilkie" in France, 1917.

Madeleine, Frederick Hugh, Joan, and Peter.

scale for the first time. The British employed four hundred with great success, a lesson soon forgotten by the allies to their sorrow in 1940.

At the beginning of 1918 there was little indication of the end of the war. The Germans began transporting armies from the eastern front where they were now no longer needed because of the Russian collapse. This gave both sides a breathing space to consolidate positions and to prepare for the spring offensive. It was the origin of the laconic comment, "All quiet on the western front." Foch was to be commander-in-chief of all the allied forces; in his counter offensive he was to throw in large numbers of Americans eager for the fray. On 21 March the long expected German attack began first against the British, retaking ground won earlier at heavy costs and penetrating some forty miles through British lines. The French line was also breached, and Paris was once again threatened. But the line held, and in July the allies including the Americans counter attacked using tanks. It was to be the beginning of the end. The battle of Amiens opened on 8 August, a date which Ludendorff later called "a black day for Germany." Areas won and lost in the past were now to be taken for the last time in a general allied plan to overcome the Hindenberg line.

At Amiens Fred was busily engaged, as he had been since his leave to England the preceding September. He continued to accept whatever challenge came his way with cheerfulness and could be depended upon to volunteer without hesitation. Never interested in a commission he did however become a Lance Corporal, a rank in which he distinguished himself by his qualities of leadership, as well as the fine example he set. A second time he was cited for bravery; the official citation reads: *Bar to Military Medal*. In front of Vis-on-artois on the night of 1st/2nd September 1918. He was Non Commissioned Officer in charge of a section of four men, and responsible for communication from brigade headquarters to a forward report centre. He was continually out between these points repairing broken lines and at all times showed the greatest bravery and devotion to duty. He set a splendid example to his section and it was largely through his efforts that communication was maintained through a heavily shelled area, thereby enabling the final assembly to be successfully completed." Diltz writes, "I believe that then and since the war Wilkie was prepared in every way to give up his life. He had no fear and was absolutely dedicated to the cause."

Once more sadness was to enter his life; word came that his mother was dying. It was just a year since Harold's death, and this news must have been terribly hard to hear. Yet he betrayed no weakness of spirit, and when a British staff officer came to him with an offer of compassionate leave in England, he refused.

He was to reach England sooner than he thought; the war for him was almost over. A great British attack was launched on 27 September in which Fred and his companions participated. The German fire was extremely heavy, and some of it struck Fred. In the action at Bourlon Wood he was wounded in the hand, arm, and leg by shrapnel. Still able to walk he was bandaged and sent to the rear. For the third time he was decorated in the field. The citation reads: "*Second Bar to Military Medal.* Near Inchy-en-Arois September 27th, 1918 for outstanding example and devotion to duty. This NCO was in charge of a party of brigade linesmen responsible for communications to brigade headquarters. During the assembly previous to the attack the lines were frequently out, but realizing the most urgent need of maintaining communication and though exposed to heavy enemy shellfire, by his example of inspiration to the men of his command, breaks were rapidly repaired and communication maintained. In the subsequent advance he was repeatedly exposed to heavy enemy machine gun fire and shell fire, but worked throughout two days and nights without sleep until wounded on the night of twenty-eighth September.

The efforts of this NCO contributed in a large degree to the successful maintenance of signal communication at a time when it was most important."

It is claimed by some that he was recommended for the VC (Victoria Cross) but was given instead the third MM (Military Medal). As there are no records of recommendations we shall never know; Fred himself never discussed it and was acutely embarrassed when it was mentioned. It is true, however, that he is the only Canadian to emerge from both World Wars with three military medals. His first reaction when wounded was, "Will I ever be able to play again," but fortunately on arrival at Reading Hospital in England it was found that none of the wounds was serious. After some weeks in hospital he was transferred for convalescence to Epsom on 12 December and was able to worship at St Paul's in London on Christmas Day. From Epsom he was sent to embarkation camp at Rhyl in Wales, where he was to remain until 23 February 1919, when he boarded the *SS Belgic* for Halifax. In retirement he made a sentimental journey back to this place in Wales where during his convalescence he had walked every Sunday to service at St Asaph Cathedral some ten kilometers away.

His sister Ruth says, "I can still remember the day he returned from overseas, sitting in father's study; he kept saying in his deep voice, "It's too good to be true." He had experienced two and a half years of agony and danger which most men did not expect to survive. He had lived through more than most men live in a lifetime, and he had returned to a home without a mother and a brother. He was discharged on 27 March 1919; his pay had been $1.15 a day. His height was 5' 11½"; he had grown two inches since enlistment. His age was twenty-two.

THE PREPARATION

The joy of homecoming was tempered by the obvious changes that had taken place. Within walking distance of the family house lay buried both his mother and brother, and it was to their graves that he made an early pilgrimage.

The transition from war to peace is never easy; the structured routine of day to day existence is replaced with the problem of holding a steady job and providing shelter and sustenance for self and a family. And jobs were hard to find. Veterans after World War I had to compete with an army of workers now on the labour market as a result of the shutting down of munitions factories. Fred remembered many of his comrades who, having served their country well, were now trudging the streets looking for work or even a place to live. For years home building had ceased, to the dismay of thousands of veterans who had chosen to remain in Toronto rather than return to the farms and villages from which they had enlisted. Many of these men had left home single but were now married with children and desperately needed living space. Because of the demand, prices were high; scores applied for every vacancy, and families had to double up.

My family came to Toronto in 1921 when, as my mother put it, "You couldn't get a house for love or money." She finally did, in an older section of Cabbagetown, by paying rent in advance and to the agent a sum of money described as "good will." The first night we discovered the house was vermin infested, and we ended up sleeping on the street. In view of the fact that seven of us were children we were lucky to get even this. I remember the story of a doughty lady who heard of a house being rented near Riverdale Park. Dashing there she left her five young ones to play close by in the cemetery. When her turn came to be interviewed, the first question was, "Have you any children?" She replied, "I have five children in there," pointing to the cemetery. She got the house and managed to hold it for some years.

The veterans of World War II returned to find that effort and plans had been made to absorb them back into society in a rightful and honoured place. Positions were held for them with seniority, all increments during their absence accruing to them automatically. Grants of cash were paid to each man on demobilization, and grants for land, buildings, or education were also available. Nothing like this was even dreamed at the time of World War I, and the result for some years was chaotic. For most of the men higher education was out of the question in those days. Although the fees were ridiculously cheap by to-day's standards, it was simply not possible for the average student to pay them, let alone study for seven months without some form of income, unless there was a father's support available, which was fortunately the case with Fred. Although a clergyman's stipend was low in view of the education and qualifications required, yet with a free house and utilities it was still above that of the average working man, and a higher education was within reach of children of the clergy. In fact, by scrimping and saving, the clergy usually provided as much academic training as other professions did for their children. The two Wilkinson girls Jean and Ruth attended Havergal College; Heber was preparing for his college career in the family manner, by doing a two year stint with the Bell Telephone Company prior to his attending university. All four children were to turn out well and display leadership ability in the communities where they lived: Jean in England and Toronto, Ruth in Montreal, Heber in India, and Fred of course in Toronto.

Fred lost no time in returning to his first love, and the piano rang out as of old in the early morning hours, to the delight of all in the house. Later in the day he could be found seated at the organ in the church, where Heber or one of the girls would be sent to fetch him for supper. Often his father would slip into a pew and revel in the joy of a son come home as he listened to his playing, something that Fred could not seem to get enough of as he tried to compensate for all he had missed over nearly three years.

He had not told anyone about the resolution made after the loss of his brother, but it must have been a wonderful moment for his father when shortly after his return Fred told him that he proposed to take Harold's place in the ministry. He went to University College to enroll for a second year in arts; the fees were forty dollars for each of the first and second years and thirty five dollars for the third year. At the same time he registered in Wycliffe College as a resident with the intention of doing some pre-theological training along with his university studies. There were no fees for theological students because of the generosity of founders and supporters; and although students in theology had to live in, these costs were somewhat offset through bursaries and grants.

Senator Walker renewed his contact with Fred almost immediately after Fred's return from overseas and saw him regularly at the church. "He didn't seem to worry about anything, not even his own career. After the war he didn't have a care in the world, although he got more serious later on. He came back unscathed; some came back with a hangover from the war, but not Fred." He certainly plunged into new as well as old activities; in addition to performing on the piano or organ at every opportunity, he began to teach in order to augment his income. Grace MacDonald remembers her late husband Percy having his first organ lessons with Fred, who later passed him on to Dr H.A. Fricker for further studies. Fricker had come from England to be the organist at Metropolitan Church — Lillian Massey had endowed the position with the proviso that the occupant possess an FRCO (Fellow of the Royal College of Organists) — he was also to become conductor of the Mendelssohn choir and one of Canada's best known musicians. Fricker was successor to Whealdon, who was Fred's teacher and mentor before the war; his impress was so great that Fred would make public reference to his kindness some fifty years later.

Fred was appointed university organist and choir master, a position he was to occupy with distinction for some four years, during which he managed to present a number of famous choral works and perform organ recitals of merit. Canon Arthur Smith says, "I can remember many comments from women who were contemporaries, about this very handsome young man who played the organ in Convocation Hall." One of these ladies was Kate Calvert, the widow of the late George Calvert, who became Bishop of Calgary. She entered the university in the fall of 1920, when the men were returning to university after serving overseas, and it was then that she met her future husband and through him, Fred. She writes, "The university did a great service for the students when famous preachers from all parts of the world were invited to preach in Convocation Hall on Sunday morning, for which Fred played the organ." Many services, concerts, and recitals, all being well attended, took place there during the university year.

Commercial entertainment was still in its infancy, and much of it was suspect if not ostracized as undesirable. Harry Maude was one of the leaders of the young people at St Peters in the post-war years. He recalls making plans to show a Charlie Chaplin movie in the parish hall: "The rector (Fred's father) called me on the telephone. 'You are advertising a film — some actor man'. The upshot was that he wouldn't let us show it." This was not as unexpected at the time as one might think, although the signs of change were evident. Movie houses were opening everywhere, and they were cheap. Small houses charged 25 or 15 cents for admission, and this continued for some years. Quite good pieces of china were later given away with every admission; at Saturday matinees children were admitted for 5 cents, and each child received a piece of candy. The program would include a segment or two of a serial popularly called a "cliff hanger," where the hero or heroine would remain poised in danger until the next week. The feature film would star one of the new movie idols. About this time I remember seeing *Annie Laurie*, a magnificent movie. There was a romantic air about the movie houses, magic and unbelievable, the atmosphere made vivid by a pianist and violinist playing appropriate music. New forms of dance like the Charleston and the Fox Trot began to appear, and dance halls sprang up in several places; soon the big name bands came to grace the new hedonistic age. Unlike post World War II, the churches in the 1920s still held the loyalty of most people. On the street where we lived in Cabbagetown there was only one family that did not walk out to church on Sunday morning.

The largest congregations still came in the evenings, although the mornings were well attended; every church held Sunday school in the afternoon at 3 pm. The Anglican Church boasted the highest attendance and prestige; most citizens were of British background. In those days there were not many other ethnic groups in the city. Every Sunday, if not playing at the university, Fred would assist his father in some way, and in the afternoon he would teach a young men's Bible class. Often on a week night or Saturday he would invite some of these young men to Wycliffe College and lead them in discussion groups. Harry Maude says, "As teenagers we had great affection for him," and his wife adds, "If Fred asked them on a Saturday to visit, Harry would drop all in order to attend."

Fred's popularity was evident to all who knew him at this stage of his life. He found time to participate in squash and tennis, and to play on a rugby and hockey team. In the summers he worked in mission churches on the prairies, mainly in the Diocese of Athabasca in northern Alberta. This was an experience he valued, learning much from the fine families to whom he ministered; and when his sister Jean stopped by, he proudly showed her the little church he had painted.

In Toronto on Sunday evenings after church young people still gathered in people's homes, and at one of these gatherings in the rectory Fred met Jean's girl friend Madeleine Harkness, who was to become his love and his wife. They were well matched; her sense of dedication, high ideals, and charm were so evident that one felt drawn to her as though an old friend or confidant. Gentle and incapable of speaking or acting harshly, she was cultured, educated, and a good musician. It was very much love at first sight, and soon the two were inseparable, even to sharing the organ bench at Convocation Hall. Some can distinctly remember her appearance beside him on the bench turning pages during recitals. As one person observed, "They went so well together!" Some who knew Fred's mother have remarked on how much alike she and Madeleine were; how often this comparison can be made! Madeleine acquired a host of admirers who regarded her with enduring respect and affection.

It was about this time that Bert Diltz, Fred's comrade in France, decided to attend an organ recital in Convocation Hall. Climbing the many stairs to his seat he thought on those days in Europe when life was cheap and there seemed no end of death and destruction. And yet here he was listening to the great D minor prelude and fugue of Bach, played by his trench mate. "What a feeling it was to see that fellow I knew at the Somme sitting there with a gown on and playing the great organ." Fred was to continue these duties until the spring of 1924 when he reached the end of his academic schooling. Having received a BA in 1922, he spent the next two years reading theology, including Hebrew and Greek, which gave him a Licentiate in Theology in 1924. In the spring of that year he also received his MA, and on the Sunday morning of 27 April he knelt before Bishop Robins of Athabasca to be ordained deacon in the Church of the Ascension in Hamilton Ontario.

Robins had been invited by Bishop Clark of Niagara to perform the ordination because Fred had worked for him during the three preceeding summers on the prairies, Hamilton is the see city of the Diocese of Niagara. And the Church of the Ascension was chosen for the ordination because Fred was to begin his curacy there under the direction of Robert Renison, its famous rector. It is strange how the paths of these two would cross in the years ahead: Fred to succeed Renison as rector in Vancouver and again later as rector of St Pauls in Toronto, Renison to go on to become Archbishop and Metropolitan of Ontario before whom Fred would kneel again nearly thirty years later to be consecrated Coadjutor Bishop of Toronto. The excitement of graduation and ordination was heightened by the news of the engagement of Fred and Madeleine. For the summer months he would dash back to Toronto whenever possible to spend an evening with her at some concert or recital, and on Saturday 30 September, amid a downpour of rain, the two were united in marriage by the Reverend T. R. O'Meara, principal of Wycliffe College, in St Peters Church in Toronto. They settled in Hamilton for what was to be a short ministry, lasting just fifteen months but made memorable by the arrival of their son Peter on 24 August 1925.

In the same summer of 1925 Fred agreed to act for four months as priest in charge of St Anne's Church in Toronto, during the absence of its rector. It is interesting that this was his first charge and that when he was bishop in the late 1950s he had to face a decision as to whether or not to close this same church. Instead he asked me to go there as priest in charge. It was in this same church that he celebrated his last service of Holy Communion at the marriage of my son in September 1980.

THE ROAD WEST

In October Fred, with Madeleine and young Peter, left Hamilton for the city of Saskatoon and Emmanuel Theological College, where at the invitation of Dr Hallam, the principal, Fred became professor of Old Testament. It was often said that a clergyman with ambition for higher office should go west, and many who did were ultimately called back east in due time to take charge of large churches and often dioceses. Certainly Fred was one of these, although in his case the road west was not paved with promotions. But all who knew him in those days are quick to point out that promotions seemed to hold no interest for him. What did interest him, however, was the opportunity to continue the work he had begun with his Bible class at St Peter's in Toronto, and to teach the scriptures to young clergymen on a full-time basis. At the age of twenty nine he was young for such an appointment, but his war time experience, to say nothing of his obvious ability in dealing with men during his Wycliffe and university life, compensated for his relative youth. Hallam obviously knew his man.

The Wilkinsons occupied the ground floor of a large house called the college annex, which was some two blocks from the college building. Canon Watts remembers how in 1925 the arrival of Professor Wilkinson coincided with his own first year in the college as a theological student. "He was one of our well respected teachers, and we were sorry to lose him to St Stephen's in Calgary" in 1928.

Above the Wilkinsons lived at least a dozen students, some of whom came to be baby sitters for them. Fred loved teaching and was obviously in love with his subject. "He was professor of Old Testament when I entered the college in 1925. I was always grateful to him because he was a good teacher and made the Old Testament live for me"; this from Wilfred Wilkinson (no relation), retired Bishop of Brandon. Stanley Steer, retired Bishop of Saskatoon, remembers Fred and Madeleine playing duets on the piano for the students, as well as extending hospitality to them. According to Bishop Steer, Fred expected discipline and got it, a view echoed by Bishop Wilfred Wilkinson: "He was well liked by the students and fair in his dealings with them. He had been in the army, and the officer and other rank relationships were carried over to the college." This did not prevent him, however, from accompanying one of his students Ray Horsefield into town to help him select a "whoopee" skirt for his wife who was ill. The former remembers Fred's amusement at the absurdity of two hefty clerics shopping for a whoopee skirt. Walter Barfoot, later to become Primate of the Canadian church, was a friend of Fred and now also a fellow professor on the staff at Emmanuel; he often would baby sit Peter. It was a happy time for these old friends, but it came to an end when Fred agreed to become the rector of St Stephen's Church in Calgary. There was no dissatisfaction on his part with his post at Emmanuel, but unless he was going to make a career of academic teaching, three terms was enough. He wanted the challenge of administration and the excitement of parish life. So in the spring of 1928 the family moved into their first rectory.

Here it was that he settled into the pastoral life of the church, for up until now he had only experienced a brief curacy in Hamilton, the short interim charge at St Anne's for the summer, and the term of teaching at Emmanuel. In his first parish he was sole custodian of the souls of men and women, and for the first time he had to make decisions affecting the lives of people, an awesome responsibility. Bishop Steer remarks, "I found Fred Wilkinson most friendly and encouraging, and I had great admiration for him," a view held by all who came under his influence either as student or parishioner in those early days of his ministry in the west. The word *encouraging* is significant, for in all his dealings with people throughout his long life, he imparted courage most naturally. He found parish life, particularly visiting which is a vital part of ministry, extremely gratifying. Organizing groups and effective committees, an area in which he was to become expert in later years, formed a part of his new duties. Kate Calvert comments, "Fred is still remembered with great affection; and where they still say, 'He could make the organ speak,' the same Casavant instrument is in use today." By now he was exchanging letters with his brother Heber, who after his ordination in 1926 had agreed to serve the missionary society of the church of India. Prior to his departure for that country Heber had married Rowena Stringer, one of the Havergal girls who worshipped at St Peter's in those days before the war. Their honeymoon was the long journey to India where they were to remain in a most successful ministry for almost thirty years.

Calgary is associated with the second great event in the life of the family, for on 29 June 1929 as the people of St Stephen's prepared to celebrate the parish picnic, a daughter Joan Madeleine was born into the Wilkinson family. It was a busy period in the life of the new mother; her hands were full managing a new baby and an active three year old son, with a husband fully occupied in parish duties every day and most evenings.

Four years is not long in a new post, but it was to be the end of Fred's sojourn in Calgary. In 1932 he accepted the rectorship and became sub-dean of Christ Church Cathedral in Vancouver. The bishop of the diocese was also the dean in this case, which meant he retained control of the cathedral. It would seem that Fred's career was destined to advance quickly: little more than a year of curacy, three as an academic teacher, four in his first parish, and four in Vancouver, his second parish — all considerably less than the average clerical tenure, a record not likely to instill confidence in those looking for a leader and pastor. Bishop Renison had recommended him on at least two occasions.

He arrived in Vancouver amidst the great depression. "Times were tough" was a familiar saying, and the west was suffering along with the rest of North America. It was the migrant stage, and men "rode the rails" from one end of the country to the other in search of work on the prairies, in logging camps, or in the mines of the east coast. In the cities and towns thousands were unemployed and on welfare, which was then considered a disgrace, and people went to amazing lengths to earn a few dollars and stay off relief. The churches became involved in providing additional assistance in order to augment welfare payments, which of course were never enough. Hundreds of hampers were sent by churches to needy families at Christmas and other times. Most recipients were not members of the church or rarely if ever attended, and meeting their needs became increasingly difficult as Sunday offerings decreased.

For Fred the experience of coping with want had begun in Calgary, but now the demand had risen to alarming proportions particularly at churches like the Cathedral; situated in the downtown areas they were the target of many migrants. The thought of people begging for work and food caused Fred great distress, and the memory of that bleak time was to remain with him long after. He once told me he often saw the same faces in Vancouver that he had seen in Calgary, people looking for handouts. He did his utmost for all, even the "professionals." Don Knight, a cathedral parishoner, remembers a group going into the Cathedral on one occasion, and Fred telling them to go ahead, he would catch up with them later, as he stopped to give some fellow money.

He was becoming widely known in the west through the medium of radio. Every Sunday evening he would broadcast from the cathedral, and the program met with much approval.

This was a new ministry for churches in key places across the country, and everywhere it was welcomed. The only negative reaction Fred received was when he announced his title on one occasion as "The Necessity of Disciplined Life." In a slip of the tongue he substituted "wife" for "life," and although he corrected himself, he still received letters of protest. Such was the power of radio in those early days.

Peter Kaye, who arrived with his bride from England about this time and became a sidesman, remembers Fred and Madeleine as genial and hospitable friends, Fred giving strong leadership both at the cathedral and in community affairs. The interior of the cathedral was poorly lighted, and in order to improve this Fred set up a committee to oversee new work and also to rebuild the crypt. Marean Swan says that Fred "extended the chancel into a beautiful chancel and sanctuary" which apparently was needed, for she says that in earlier days old timers referred to the cathedral as "the road house." Archdeacon Swanson remembers in particular the reconstruction of the crypt; it was a big job, but he says it made a very good useable area below the church. At a time when money was scarce and similiar projects were being shelved, all agreed that the renovation program was a courageous step and a tribute to Fred's energy, initiative, and faith.

Peter Kaye remembers Fred as being "firm but sympathetic" in dealing with a petty theft at the cathedral, and this is also the impression of Gordon Adam, a playmate of Peter and Joan. "As a boy I remember Fred Wilkinson as a warm, friendly person. I remember the mildness of a well merited rebuke for a childish escapade. Peter, Joan, and I 'borrowed' a string of pearls belonging to their mother and buried them in the Wilkinson garden, presumably in the expectation of magic! They were eventually unearthed and restored to their owner, but it was left to the head of the family to deal with the culprits. I expect I was the ring leader, and certainly my memory is that Fred had a more tolerant view of the misdemeanor than I would have expected from my own father." Joan had quite forgotten about this incident, but she does have vivid memories of when the same two boys locked her in the basement. This absolutely terrified her and was apparently dealt with by her father on a sterner basis. About this aspect of discipline Joan adds, "He would spank me on the botton when I did something naughty." Best of all is her memory of Vancouver "when we went on terrific picnics with cookouts. Father was great on picnics. It was at this time that I learned to row, when we rented a cottage at a place called Half Moon Bay. Father owned an old four-door Ford in which he and mother would drive to Bellingham, Washington occasionally." As in Calgary they entertained continually; a guest always being present for most meals. As in later years this is where much of Fred's money went. It has been said he was not happy in Vancouver, which seems strange in view of the magnificence of the city. His family was not aware of any discontent, but after four years it was time to move on.

MONTREAL

To the east and the Church of St James the Apostle in Montreal
the Wilkinsons headed in 1936 after eleven years in western
Canada. Here they would remain for eight years, perhaps the
happiest of Fred's parish ministry. St James was a distinguished
parish on St Catherine Street in the heart of downtown Montreal. It was built in 1864, and the city had grown around it. It
had known but two rectors, both with long records in office,
before Fred arrived. No one knows exactly why he chose to
move from a cathedral to a parish church so distant. Had he
stayed in Vancouver he certainly would have been front runner in the next episcopal election, but he seemed not to be interested. The move did bring him closer to friends and relations in
Toronto and to his sister in Montreal. One wonders how his
name could appear on a list of candidates for a post in far away
Montreal, however well known he was on the west coast.
Large parishes, however, often have strong preferences for
men of a particular background or even country. Of six rectors
of St James the Apostle, Fred and four others were from Nova
Scotia. Undoubtedly too, Bishop Farthing of Montreal knew
Fred; certainly in later years Fred spoke of him in the most
glowing terms, saying how much he had learned from him.

On their arrival they were ensconsed in the Windsor Hotel
to await the decoration of the rectory. Their new home was to
be the first and only problem of any consequence in the new

parish. The rectory was beside the church and faced directly onto St Catherine Street. Joan and Peter would hang out the upstairs windows watching the action on the street below. Prostitution thrived, and panhandlers and "winos" loitered around the front doorstep. The constant noise of trolley cars and fire engines threatened to drive them all crazy. The kitchen was in the basement, and food had to be sent upstairs by means of a lift. It was soon apparent to all that this could not continue. Fred met with the wardens, and they agreed to find a new house; eventually the old rectory was torn down.

Except for this problem, which was rectified in a few months, their stay in Montreal was everything they could wish for. Fred's sister Jean says, "Montreal was a happy time," a view echoed by Joan who adds, "Montreal was really exciting." She was seven on their arrival and fifteen when they left. As a parent Fred was very much like his father, Joan recalls, "He was strict — must do that, couldn't do this — Sunday was taboo for everything. He was a strong figure but very considerate of mother. He had the final word, usually making the decision regarding the children and the family. In Montreal he would walk me to school and pick me up in the afternoon. We were very close even though we had battles, but whenever he went away he always brought us something back." Jean agrees, "He was the leader, the father figure, but went out of his way to please Madeleine and was very devoted to his children."

Once again Fred's organizing ability came to the fore. Shortly after his arrival he formed an Advisory Board of men from the congregation, and the architect Ross Wiggs became the chairman of the building committee. He writes, "Fred had the happy faculty of picking prominent businessmen, who ordinarily took little interest in church matters, to serve on various committees, and it proved very successful. He and Madeleine brought new life to the church because their friendliness drew people to them." It was a delight for Fred to find Harry Maude, one of his Bible class boys from Toronto, now living in Montreal and a member of St James where he was bass soloist and recitalist. Harry was overjoyed with his new rector, who on one occasion, when a cipher developed in the organ before an important wedding, removed his cassock, climbed into the organ chamber, and fixed it. He remembers fine organ recitals given by Fred and the organist; from time to time Fred would have a piano placed in the chancel and give a recital after Evensong. Harry remarks on the way Fred worked on ecumenism, remembering particularly that he invited a Russian Orthodox choir in on several Good Fridays with great success. He was beginning to be in demand as a speaker, was widely quoted in the press, and was highly regarded in all quarters for his forthright manner and warm personality. The Wilkinson's welcomed visitors as usual, and gave frequent lunches and receptions, a custom they were to continue and greatly expand later in Toronto. Gordon Adam, a friend of Peter and Joan from Vancouver, writes, "The family relationship continued when the Wilkinsons moved to St James in Montreal in the late thirties, and I remember as a boy our staying with them when we crossed the Atlantic and back, from Montreal to the north of Ireland, where we spent alternate summers with my mother's family outside Belfast."

On 30 August 1942 Fred's father died at the age of eighty-two in Toronto, and the family journeyed from Montreal for the funeral. Fred Wilkinson senior had been retired for some years, but had remained active and was well liked by his new neighbours in north Toronto and the parish of St Timothy where he now worshipped. Reg Soward remembers him seated near the back of the church leaning on his cane, taking everything in. One lady recalls that whenever the old gentleman took a wedding he would give her the fee. Although he took to smoking a pipe, he still insisted on his old standards both for himself and others. He continued to be proud of his sons. In the archives of the University of Toronto is his neat letter stating that Fred had received official conformation of his awards and decorations. Harold's funeral, which Senator Walker found so impressive, would not have been so except for the same father's insistence that it be conducted in proper military fashion. Because Fred was the most like his father — the two saw eye to eye on many things — he felt he had lost a friend and spoke of this in later years. On one occasion he remarked, "I shall never forget the solemn and beautiful way in which my father conducted the Holy Communion at eight o'clock on Sunday mornings." With his passing went much that was precious in the life of a community. Archdeacon Swanson writes, "He was one of the last definite Wycliffe men. With increasing tolerance there came a different type of parson, and from what I hear this is the new breed and we had better get used to them." For nearly forty years he had put his stamp for good on the religious life of Toronto. How it would have delighted his heart to know that within a year his son would return to that city where his name would become honoured by those of all faiths and of every denomination for almost the next thirty-seven years.

It is possible that when Fred was in Toronto Bishop Renison indicated his intentions of going to the Diocese of Moosonee as its bishop the following year, leaving St Pauls Church without a rector. To fill this vacancy a committee of distinguished men of St Pauls met for sometime considering a list of names submitted by Archbishop Owen, then Bishop of Toronto. The list suggested a number of estimable men including several from outside Canada. Outstanding ability was needed to preside over this parish of prestige, influence, and affluence. Canon Cody, known to those in Britain and the United States as Cody of St Pauls, was the great genius who built St Pauls on Bloor Street. After many years as rector he retired and was appointed president of the University of Toronto, a post in which he was eminently successful; later he served as chancellor of the same university. At the time of his resignation he was succeeded by Bishop Renison, a charming and eloquent Irishman known across Canada as an outstanding speaker and writer. Renison was a mystic, like many of his countrymen, and the possessor of a brilliant philosophical mind; his articles appeared in the Wednesday issues of the Toronto *Globe and Mail*. He had been Fred's first rector after his ordination and preceded Fred at the Cathedral in Vancouver. From Vancouver he went to the Diocese of Athabasca and was consecrated as its bishop; from there he came to St Pauls. He had accepted the call to St Pauls because he felt keenly that he might better serve by preaching to a large audience of several thousand people each week, but now felt he should accept the call to go to the north country and into the mission field once again. It follows that having a warm and affectionate regard for Fred he would most strongly recommend that he succeed him.

Strangely Fred did not want to leave Montreal, nor did any of the family. Joan says, "I came to Toronto with a bad feeling." Fred was apprehensive of the political pressures associated with a very large parish. To succeed two powerful predecessors was to walk in their shadow; at least he felt this way, and really did not look forward to Toronto. He asked Archbishop Owen to call on Archdeacon Swanson, who in fact was some years later to succeed him at St Pauls. Colonel Robertson in Montreal urged Fred to go for what was to be a wider ministry, as did Bishop Renison of course, and to those voices Archbishop Owen of Toronto added his own strong endorsement. The committee from St Paul's visited with Fred and one man asked about his wife. Fred replied, "My wife is my wife," which seemed to set things in proper order for the remainder of the interview. They asked him formally to become their rector, and he finally agreed. Early in the New Year the family said goodbye to their many friends and boarded the train for Toronto, not one of them looking forward to the new experience.

ST PAUL'S

On Sunday 23 January 1944 at eleven in the morning Fred Wilkinson was inducted as rector of St Pauls by the Most Reverend Derwyn Owen, Archbishop of Toronto and Primate of All Canada. He came as chief pastor to the place where in 1913 he had virtually begun as a young musician, scrambling over the pipes of the new organ as it was being installed. St Pauls is one of the great institutions in Canadian church life. It is the scene of many national gatherings, perhaps because of its size — seating over 3,000 — as well as its Gothic beauty. But it is also a parish church with a large congregation of devoted and dedicated workers, who by their witness and stewardship contribute much to the life of the city and beyond. It is the highest honour to be the rector of such a church, but it was for a long time a dubious one for Fred. He was right in his earlier apprehension of the devotees of his two famous predecessors — the "Codyites" and "Renisonites"; as he called them — in whose eyes he could do nothing right. Knowing Fred it is hard to believe that a warden would make life so difficult that "I had to carry him along as best I could; the fellow simply wouldn't co-operate." In spite of this Fred generously appointed Canon Cody the rector emeritus of St Paul's.

As usual Fred's finances were not healthy; he apparently did not drive much of a bargain in salary and allowances. The parish had never owned a rectory; Fred had to sell his car to raise a down payment for a house on Roxborough Street and found it increasingly difficult to pay the mortgage and taxes. Eventually because he needed the money, he was forced to sell the house to the church for what he paid for it, $9,000. It seems a hard bargain, but he was never concerned about his own needs. His sister Jean remarked, "He never asked for anything at St Pauls or elsewhere for himself; he was never demanding of anything for himself." The house is still the rectory, and as I sat recently on the veranda with Canon Dann, the present rector, he recalled that Fred had "painted this house outside right to the top."

In 1952 Joan married John Hoolihan, a young and promising lawyer, and the two set up house on the third floor of the rectory. This was a benefit to a young couple starting out, but it was also a bonus for Fred, who had for some time been using public transportation. He now had access to his son-in-law's car, an arrangement that continued for a year and provided some hilarious moments. Once Fred backed the car out of the driveway and over a suitcase containing his robes.

Shortly after the family arrived in Toronto, Peter announced his intention to enlist. The parents tried to dissuade him: he was still young and needed to complete his education. But in the fashion of youth he had his way and like his father enlisted as a private, but with the Royal Regiment of Canada. He went overseas in October 1944, saw action in north west Europe, and received a leg wound in Holland. Jack Clough recalls seeing Peter in hospital in England and then writing to Fred: "I remember from then on how prompt Fred always was in replying to letters written to him. It is an admirable trait, not only politeness but also a sign of grace." After convalescence Peter returned home in the summer of 1945 and enrolled in Toronto University where he received his Master of Arts. He later graduated from Wycliffe College, and served a curacy with his father at St Pauls. It is interesting how his career seems to parallel his fathers; currently he is a popular professor of philosophy at the University of Windsor, Ontario.

While Fred worked at pleasing the "old guard" at St Pauls and coping with his finances, he kept his own counsel so that few knew about these problems, and both were resolved. He gave every appearance of being the man in charge. Reg Stackhouse speaks of the times he met Fred: "The first occasion was when he appeared at St Pauls at a military service shortly after he had taken over. He looked every inch the person to be doing it; he was robust, erect, dark mustached. He seemed every inch the CO on parade. I remember one service on Easter evening when he referred to World War I and how he and his comrades were in the trenches with all the misery and death. Standing there looking over the parapet they noticed a bird which they watched; it gave them a sense of hope that life was more than what was going on around them. He had that capacity as a preacher to draw on the personal as well as the profound. It was worth going to hear; it was a testimony to him as a preacher that the attendances were so impressive."

It was a special pleasure for Fred when ten of his old comrades gathered together one Sunday evening to hear and see him again. Harry Tonkin, the man beside Fred when he got his first Military Medal, remembers that Sunday evening service "when Fred, recognizing us, mentioned during the announcements the presence of his old comrades who had come to honour him." Bert Diltz who was also there, says that "one of our fellows who could neither read nor write stood at attention during the singing of the hymns." Fred was as glad to see his old comrades as they were to see him; indeed, all his life he would go out of his way to greet or spend time with any military man. The bond forged under wartime circumstances seems to transcend every difference and becomes stronger with the passing years. Charles Dalton expresses it in a saying popular in the ranks: "I trust implicitly in the man on my right and my left," because, of course, so often one's life depend on them. It gave Fred the greatest of pleasure when the Queen's Own Rifles asked him to be their chaplain. He accepted with alacrity, never missing a parade night if he could help it, visiting the messes of all ranks equally. The men of the regiment of every rank held him in very high regard, respect, and affection, according to Jack Clough, who served with the regiment overseas and succeeded him as chaplain when Fred became bishop.

All his genius for organization could be felt in the administration of this huge parish. Dick Newsham, his curate, was deeply impressed with this ability in his rector: "He was a fabulous man for organization; he identified with all the youth groups. We organized a camp for the poorer children in the neighbourhood. To see a corporation lawyer scrubbing a kid down in a tub with soap was quite an experience." He goes on to say, "We had three wolf cub packs, about one hundred kids, who on one occasion brought their fathers along for a meal together. Fred was to be inducted into the pack, and I asked him how we should handle it. He replied that he would be inducted as if he were an ordinary boy. At the ceremony we put on him a wolf pack hat, scarf, etc.; he didn't lose one inch of dignity."

Ken Scott went as curate to St Paul's in 1952. When with some hesitation and embarrassment he suggested the stipend he would require, "Fred treated my answer with scorn — 'You can't possibly support a wife and two children on that' — going on to name a figure $500 above that which I had suggested. We agreed on this, which he later confirmed in writing, only now my stipend was to be another $500 above that on which he had previously insisted." Some years later Ken said it was the first job he had ever had involving two raises before he even started work. Ken speaks feelingly of the generosity and kindness of Fred in also making him take three weeks holiday with pay, after only having worked at St Paul's for a month.

Both Scott and Newsham stress the way in which he trained his curates, giving them assignments and not interfering. If they fell down he would let them know, but never in an unkindly way. Scott says, "I think the most flattering thing about working for him was that he would give you a job to do and he would leave you alone to do it in your own way. He would never check up on you or tell you how to do it. In other words he trusted you. What higher compliment can one person pay another?" Scott goes on to say, "He was almost fiercely intolerant of any act bordering on discourtesy, even if the act was unintentional." On one occasion he opened the rector's study door to permit entrance to the Primate who was carrying his own bag. The rector strode forward to take the bag, and Ken received an appropriate dressing down. He retreated to lick his wounds, and vowed to carry every and all bags of great and small hence forward. The following day Fred asked Ken to lunch. During the course of the meal nothing was said of the incident the previous evening. Instead, Ken says, "He took me into his confidence about a number of problems he had when he first arrived at St Pauls. He let his hair down, as the saying is, and I felt flattered that a man of his eminence in the church should look upon me, a lowly deacon, as his confidant. He also astonished me after lunch by helping me on with my coat as though I were a distinguished guest. I had many an occasion to be amazed at the breadth of his firmness and of his kindness; I inevitably came to love the man."

There were a great many demands on his time not only in the parish but increasingly in the city and also the diocese. Harry Hilchey speaks of how impressed he was with Fred's keen interest and supporting the diocesan board of religious education, on which they both served. Fred was firmly convinced that the future depended on an early and sound grounding in religious knowledge. This was his own experience in his father's home, and it was what he had sought to impart in his ministry. To promote religious education Dick Newsham says, "He organized a Bible study group at which he attended as much as possible. Madeleine also attended and took an active part, she always had a contribution prepared and spoke from a personal witness point of view."

Jack Clough was made head of the committee on evangelism for the diocese. At Jack's request Fred agreed to serve on the committee and provided meeting facilities as well as breakfast. They met for many months and eventually brought Bryan Green from England to head a mission that was a tremendous success. Jack says of Fred, "He gave support from the first, generous and complete. He was always present at the meetings giving support and counsel and the warmth of his friendship." Later Jack prepared a report of some length which he sent to Fred. In no time he received a five page letter in reply with helpful comments. The completed report was later sent by Fred to the Primate, who in turn sent it far and wide to bishops and heads of colleges. It was well received, and Jack remarks, "I don't think I would have had the temerity to send it had not Fred endorsed it strongly and backed me up."

Reg Stackhouse was appointed the secretary of a commission to review the objectives of Wycliffe College; Fred was a member of this committee. Reg had to write the report, which he did in rather terse fashion, but this was not enough for a man of Fred's magnitude. "He took this small offering of mine, breathed something into it, and it turned out to be a great report. I read it and admired very much the way he made such an impressive document. We discussed it and then went on to discourse on the church and personalities he had known, none of whom he spoke disparagingly. He certainly had great men he looked up to, one being his father, another Bishop Carlyle of Montreal."

There were other less arduous demands — for example, meetings of the Queen's Own Rifles, the Canadian Legion, and the Rosedale Walking Club, a group founded in 1912 which brought together leading men in the professional and industrial world for dinner and a day of golf. Recently Carl Weber introduced me to this group, and all of the members were loud in their praise of Fred. His daughter Joan comments, "Father always enjoyed his evenings with this group."

Fred was also an exemplary neighbour. Gordon Wotherspoon lived near the Wilkinsons on Roxborough Street in Rosedale where there was a gang of bullies who used to beat up young children. Wotherspoon's son was reluctant to walk down the street to visit his cousin, but the father instructed him to do so and proceeded to follow in his car. "Just as we were passing the rectory the gang ran out of an alley and attacked my son. I jumped out of the car. Fred, who happened to be sitting on his veranda, vaulted over the railing in his clerical clothes and proceeded to give chase to the bullies. Of course, neither of us had any success as they were fleeter of foot. However, it gave my son courage and discouraged the young thugs." Fred was at this time in his early fifties and in excellent physical shape, a condition soon to change dramatically when an abcess that would not heal appeared on his thumb. It was very painful, requiring frequent medical attention, and I believe it was a fragment of shrapnel. In the strange manner of things it travelled and settled in his lower back on the kidney. He ran a fever some weeks and was very ill. Finally Fred consented to an operation. The convalescence lasted longer than the one following his original war wound in 1918.

Fred hosted the general assembly of the World council of Churches as well as the Archbishop of York in 1944 and of Canterbury in 1946. Dignitaries of church and state from many countries followed one another to St Pauls to preach or visit, and large congregations were always present. Planning and preparation for such services and functions would require considerable time, and under the circumstances a rector would often leave much of the daily routine of parish administration to his capable curates. With Fred this was certainly not the case. He carried out a planned and orderly round of personal visitations, and in the times of trouble he was the first to turn up. Dick Newsham remembers his concern for a young French Canadian boy who was a member of the cubs at St Paul's. He became very ill, and although Fred was now the bishop and no longer at St Paul's, he went faithfully to St Michael's Hospital to visit him until the lad died. Newsham adds, "If I told him about someone in need he never forgot it; he would come back later and tell me he had seen him. I remember a carpenter who lived on a laneway in St Pauls area, the houses little more than shacks. The man became very ill. Fred took communion to him every week until he died. He never knew how to play politics, and he never left a friend behind."

One of these friends was Charles Dalton the likeable commanding officer of the Queen's Own Rifles and a neighbour of Fred who saw a bit more of him than most. "He would drop in and chat with me, introducing me to a whole new concept of Christianity. For the first time I realized that there was more to it than just Christmas and Easter and a social thing. He said to me that as a soldier you were very dedicated to your men and to the cause; Christianity is the same. You can't be an honorary colonel; you are either in or out. I realized that what I had been doing was just lip service, a social thing. He really converted Helen and me to christianity."

A well known convert was the Right Honorable Roland Michener, later to become governor general of Canada, but at the time speaker of the House in Ottawa. Whenever he was in Toronto he worshipped at St Pauls. Michener recalls "He prepared me for confirmation, gave me instructions at age forty-five. He was a man of God, a cleric of unshakable faith and strong discipline."

It cannot be overlooked that this indefaticable pastor was after all a great musician and the custodian of one of the worlds finest instruments. Shortly after his arrival in 1944 Fred appointed Charles Peaker as organist. It was to be a fine arrangement, both adding their flair and imagination to concerts and recitals. Peaker was a delightful character to work with and during his preludes or postludes would on occasion throw in a few notes of a tune appropriate to some visitor he knew to be present. The two met to plan services, Fred choosing the hymns and Peaker deciding on the anthems, and music for canticles and psalms. Whenever he could Fred would go to the console and play. Dick Newsham remembers "wandering in one afternoon and the organ was going full tilt, it was Fred and Sir Ernest MacMillan playing a Bach duet." MacMillan and

Fred had similar backgrounds, both being sons of clergymen, both setting out on a career of music, both having distinguished records in World War I. MacMillan wrote musical examinations from a prisoner of war camp in Germany. Later he became the distinguished conductor of the Toronto Symphony Orchestra and the Mendelsohn Choir. Once Sir William McKie visited Fred at St Pauls and played the organ. He was for years the famous organist at Westminster Abbey. On one occasion when Fred was in England the two slipped into the Abbey in the late evening like two boys, and Fred played the great organ for McKie.

On 25 November hundreds of clergy and lay delegates of the Diocese of Toronto were called in session by Bishop Beverley to choose a Coadjutor Bishop who would succeed him on his retirement. Although Fred was a name to be reckoned with, he was by no means a sure candidate, nor is there the slightest indication that he wanted to be. There were many outstanding men in the Canadian church at the time, some of whom were already bishops, one of these and the strongest contender was Bishop Wright of Algoma. The first ballot showed Fred and he leading in that order, which surprised Fred; he had not expected to get a large number of votes. The second and third ballots were like the first, both gaining strength but neither having a majority. Fred was by now embarrassed and decided to withdraw, but some, like Jimmy Traviss, persuaded him to stay for one more ballot, to which he agreed. It was the decisive one; he was elected on the fourth ballot. With just six weeks left before his consecration, he began his farewells to the people of St Paul's, bringing to an end a dramatic and powerful ministry of eight years less one month. He was to be consecrated 6 January 1953, the same year in which his brother Heber would be consecrated Bishop of Armitsar in India. Archdeacon Swanson remarked that their father, who couldn't abide bishops, must have had grave misgivings as he looked down on two of his sons now members of that club!

THE EPISCOPATE

On the Feast of the Epiphany 6 January 1953 Fred was consecrated bishop in the church of God in St James' Cathedral by
the first rector he had served after his ordination, Archbishop
Renison, now Metropolitan Archbishop of Ontario, assisted
by the Bishops of Toronto, Niagara, Ottawa, Algoma, the
Arctic, Western New York, the Polish National Catholic
Church, the retired Bishops of Cariboo and Honan China, the
assistant Bishop of Huron, the Suffragan Bishop of Moosonee,
and in the presence of Bishop Nikon of the Russian Orthodox
Church. So to this high and ancient ecclesiastical office in the
fifty-seventh year of his life came the warrior, musician, and
priest, and it was in this role that his dedication to service
reached its highest fulfillment. In the charge to a new bishop
during his consecration these words are said: "Be to the flock of
Christ a shepherd . . . . Hold up the weak, heal the sick, bind
up the broken, bring again the outcasts, seek the lost. Be so
merciful, that you be not too remiss; so minister discipline,
that you forget not mercy." All this he viewed as a sacred trust.

As coadjutor bishop, Fred settled into a small office adjoin-
ing that of the diocesan Bishop Beverley, and there side by side
the two worked in harmony; they were both Christian
gentlemen. This arrangement was to continue for two and a

half years until Fred succeeded Bishop Beverley on 1 July 1955. Some years later, on the completion of the new diocesan centre, he dedicated its new chapel in memory of his predecessor. One of the first duties assigned to the new coadjuter bishop of Toronto was the responsibility of church extension, which had begun shortly after World War II but was experiencing difficulty keeping pace with the growth and demands of the population. The city grew outward in all directions, and the suburbs expanded rapidly, until in 1953 some thirteen amalgamated with Toronto to form a metropolitan city. New subdivisions sprang up all over "Metro" in an attempt to meet the housing demands of hundreds of thousands of new emigrants from Europe. Although many of these were not Anglican, thousands were. Adherents of the Anglican church, formerly resident in the city, were now moving to the suburbs and were looking for a new church home. This move on the part of so many was to create a new and growing problem for the downtown churches later on.

The church extension program had, as one man put it, "become moribund" primarily because there was not enough money in the new communities to do the job without help. Fred had the initiative, drive, and confidence to convince the diocesan committee that something could be done, and began by requesting authority to arrange a bank loan for the sum of $300,000. One of those present said he voted for it because he was sure Fred would never get it, but he did get it — a sizable sum in those days — by merely walking into the office of the president of one of Canada's largest banks and asking for it. Douglas Mackintosh, the secretary-treasurer of the diocese, was to be of inestimable help in launching the projects as well as handling the funds. Archdeacon Dann was made director of the program and proved to be a tower of strength to the bishop. Together Fred and Bob Dann travelled the diocese many times selecting and purchasing sites, interviewing clergy and laity, and arranging credit for the building of churches, parish halls, and rectories. Portables were also purchased, and these served as temporary places of worship until a congregation became sufficiently established and ready to erect a permanent structure.

Bob Dann says of Fred, "He would lay on a whole series of calls around the diocese, from Oshawa to Peterborough, from Orillia to Barrie, with sundry stops in between. On one occasion we started early in the morning and arrived home at 1:00 AM. I would have apples in the car, and when the day was done there wouldn't be one left. In between he would partake of candy; "Have to keep up my energy," he would say. Frequently he didn't have enough money to buy a lunch on our trips." From place to place he went leaving behind groups of enthusiastic people having no shadow of a doubt that their church was soon to become a reality. He had this ability to inspire people, not by enthusiasm but by his strength of purpose and determination and obvious sincerity. On his return to the office a long letter would be drawn up detailing all of the arrangements and affirmations of the commitments made, together with the details of the transfer of funds. Not a detail necessary to the launching of the project was omitted; not a promise was broken.

Progress on this scale requires money — a lot of it. Obviously the initial loan would soon run out. Something further had to be done; so an appeal was made by Fred to the city congregations to answer the needs of the suburbs. Many of these parishes were already feeling the pinch of dwindling congregations and increasing costs of maintenance, yet in answer to the appeal four million dollars were raised for the work of church extension. Some seventy new parishes were formed. Reg Stackhouse, who was responsible for the building of one of the new churches, says, "I think the church extension program, which saw churches erected and parishes established out of the boundaries of Metro and beyond, and which are now the greatest strength of the diocese with the exception of a few large parishes in the city, represents Fred's greatest accomplishment. It would not have happened in the dimensions that it

did, in the period that it did, without Fred. He was like a coach
with players who were good but played better because of the
leader. He gave impetus and great life to all concerned, and he
had the confidence of the business community who were
prepared to back him. The church in the era took on a new
vigour because of Fred, a vigour which it hasn't lost, not tran-
sient but still with us."

From its inception the church extension program increased
the number of parishes and missions from 184 to 259 in just ten
years. During the same period the number of clergy increased
from 280 to 389. Great credit is due to laymen and women in
the new parishes who freely gave their time and talents. While
some progress was of course to be expected in church growth
during the post-war years, the extent of the achievement was a
result of the drive and backing of Fred.

On 1 July 1955 Fred became seventh Bishop of Toronto, an
office he was to retain for eleven years. As his official residence
a fine home was purchased by the diocese on Warren Road
where many people were generously entertained in a never
ending round of receptions. Every clergyman and his wife
would be invited into the Wilkinson home during the course of
the year. The food was always excellent and ample; everything
was done to make one feel relaxed and welcomed and
esteemed. At least one social affair appeared on Fred's diary
every day. Whenever errant clergy were called in for friendly
admonition, the blow was softened by a good meal. I was one
of these. It reached his ears that I referred to him as the "boss,"
and this prompted a call from him inviting me to lunch. On my
arrival at his office he informed me of my fall from grace. I was
surprised at his reaction to the use of the term, but in later years
it made sense to me because he certainly did not see himself as a
boss at all. I suspect he really preferred to be known as the head
of a team in which everyone had some form of responsibility
and authority. At any rate the discussion was brief and to the
point, and climaxed by, "Now let's forget the whole thing and
go to lunch." During the luncheon he discoursed on many and

interesting subjects, plied me with good food, and somehow managed to convey his good opinion of me.

He had this great gift of being able to win back people he had disciplined. It was impossible to dislike him or, having been censured by him, to remain cross with him. There are some gifted people we all know in this world who can consign you to the nether regions and do it in such a way that you look forward to the journey! Dr Stackhouse, speaking of a summons he received, says, "He was the gentlest of fathers. I sat there for half an hour while he discoursed in a very general way on problems of the church, but never referring specifically to me. I remember the wisdom of his council; he was quite right, and I was the better for having listened to it. There was no suggestion of his finding fault with me or in any way chastising me." I shall always remember Bob Dann's thoughtful expression of gratitude: "I owe more to him than to any other man."

Once Dean Gilling spoke to him about a problem of one of the clergy. Obviously upset Fred responded, "I don't want you standing between me and my clergy. If a man has something to say, I want him to come to me and say it, without any in between person." Dean Gilling says, "He was concerned to get to know the clergy and help them in any way he could. He had a great heart; he was a kindly man."

All who associated with him were familiar with his strong authority, and yet none resented it in any way; they usually recognized it was the kind of leadership that was needed. Because Reg Soward was chancellor of the diocese, he was in a position to be informed about church business and any legal matters arising from clergy problems. Of Fred's leadership he says, "He was extremely good on discipline. He could be very stern but very kind and forgiving." Walter Bagnall was Bishop of Niagara during this period and a friend of Fred. The two saw much of each other, Fred delighting in the "stories" that were part of Walter's charm. Of Fred's forgiving nature, Walter says, "We worked very closely together, very honest with each other. He would discuss our own shortcomings and mistakes, but when we talked of a third person, Fred would never denounce or condemn. He would always find some redeeming feature of the fellow, even when his patience had been sorely tried."

The bishop exercised great care in clergy appointments. He was, for example, concerned not to place a man in a parish contrary to the churchmanship of that place, for he knew that such an appointment is doomed to disappointment if not failure. It was against the grain for him to hurt the sensitivities of people. Reg Stackhouse relates how Fred offered him the parish of St John's in West Toronto one morning over the telephone. "I went to see him, having decided not to accept. I was ushered into his presence, this time in his home as he was sick in bed and lay there like a whale on the beach, moving, twisting and turning, the organ-like voice rolling up from the sheets. I told him that I could not accept the appointment, which meant nothing to him; he just went on with the reasons why I should move. Looking back on it I think that I was so much putty in his hands; by the time I left with a handshake, I was the new rector of St John's. At the Induction reception I remember his suggesting to the mayor of the city that the traffic situation would be improved a lot if use was made of the ravines in Toronto. The mayor backed away from that one, saying that the conservation people would be shouting 'Hands off the ravines'. It was only a few years later that we got the Don Valley Parkway, and it is now inconceivable that Metro Toronto could function without it. It was another example of how he could think big thoughts. He always had a big vision but a practical one; he was not a dreamer but had the ability of being able to translate aspirations into actualities. Many people can dream dreams, and some can perform deeds, but it is great people that can put the two together." Jack Clough adds, "Once his mind was made up, I don't think anyone could deter him, and somehow you couldn't refuse him."

The bishop possessed a keen morality that he exercised with both sensitivity and conviction. As Colonel Dalton put it, "His sense of responsibility was such that if people did wrong, he felt that it was his duty to put them right, not that he wanted to do it, but he never shirked what was his responsibility. It had to be corrected, and it was corrected." He was much like St Paul, "as a man under authority." Because of this he exuded authority. He seemed to be larger than he was, and many people thought him well over six feet. His bearing helped in this illusion; a few people viewed it as pomposity, but they didn't really know him. The Honourable John Aird says, "Pomposity is the last word I would associate with Fred; strength and character and style is my view. It may be because he was such a large man; he had that look about him." Reg Soward refers to him "as an imposing figure"; and Lord Nugent says, "Physically he was a big man," but he was surprised on learning Fred's height.

Peter Young, for whom Fred celebrated nuptial communion and who now patrols the skys of northern Europe in a fighter aircraft, writes, "He seemed to fill the room with his presence and filled St Anne's whenever he was there. As a child he was *the* bishop in my eyes and, I thought, the only one. I was a little disappointed when I found out he wasn't. He always had a kind voice and was soft spoken to us all. His gentleness seemed to hold a strength within. As I grew older and learned of his exploits, I knew it was not imagined strength." One of his clergy Tom Rooke found him "forbidding" on first meeting but later warm and kind. "When you met him," says Bob Dann, "he struck you as pretty formidable and formal, but later no man could be more open, soldierly, friendly, and absolutely one of the boys. He knew how to maintain that balance between dignity and approachableness." Jack Clough says, "It was an education to watch him at any public gathering as he seemed to miss no one. I noted and have often seen how easily he moved from talking to notables to ordinary folk, with no change of pace or manner or attitude." He would clasp your hand at a high level simply by holding his hand up rather than down at waist level or forward as many do. This tended to bring you closer and in more intimate contact. Sometimes he would place his left hand over the handclasp, speaking a special greeting or a word of blessing. Of all the greetings I have witnessed, it was by far the most impressionable. Never was there any doubt about its sincerity.

He was the true charismatic man of the New Testament, drawing people to him and capturing their loyalty and affection. Senator Walker was quite insistent about this fact of the bishop's character: "Wherever he went he was highly regarded; he had a way of drawing men to him!" Nowhere was this more evident than among the circle of his fellow workers, where one's faults and weaknesses are easily apparent and too readily communicated. But every employee thought the world of him and gave cheerful respect to the man as well as the office. "I adored him"; one would never expect this statement from his secretary-treasurer, a salty seadog of World War II, but these are the words of Doug Mackintosh. Bishop Snell said, "He was kind, considerate, generous, and a good pastor; he really cared." Jack Clough speaks for himself as well as all the members of the Queen's Own Rifles: "Of course I was biased; I loved him as did others of the Queen's Own Rifles." This was also the feeling shared by the majority of his clergy. He tended to bring out the best in people, so that a visit with him was always an uplifting experience. No one ever came away from him without renewed strength of purpose and direction.

He gave something of himself to all who approached him. Knowledge, information, and experience was passed on where it could do the most good. Ideas and methods were suggested with such confidence that it was impossible not to be moved to action. Pat Mackay, who was the head of one of his most important committees says, "He inspired people to do more than they thought they could do. He had a presence; he was a delight to see — such confidence." Bishop Bagnall agrees: "There was something about him that gave him a presence, but it was natural. He never paraded that presence which he had naturally, and it was balanced by humility. Not everyone saw and understood that sense of humility of his." Harry Price speaks of this saying, "He was very shy about himself." Whenever the discussion turned to himself, he would seem not to hear or, with a gentle thank you, change the subject.

Norah Mitchener relates how she was assisting him to select an episcopal ring at the store of a well known Toronto jeweller. Among her many accomplishments was her knowledge of gems and settings; so it was to be expected that her selection would be superb but also expensive. Undaunted she named a figure that she felt reflected its value in view of the office of the bishop and the ecclesiastical usage of the ring. While the ensuing discussion with the jeweller could not be called haggling, the result was the same, and her suggestion of price was accepted. During all this Fred stood silently becoming more aloof and withdrawn until, when they finally left the store, he turned and said to her, "Norah, how could you?" Toward the end of his espiscopate I had the opportunity to suggest he put his thoughts on tape to use as the basis of his autobiography. The idea while appreciated was inconceivable to him; there was nothing to say that would be of the slightest interest to others. This was his appraisal of his own significance, which he reaffirmed in later years when he finally agreed to sit for a portrait. After one sitting he ran into Ken Scott who had conceived the project, and in genuine puzzlement he queried, "Why are people doing this for me?"

At a dinner which I gave for some friends one evening, General Sir Neil Ritchie, the former commander of the Eighth Army, asked if I was aware that the bishop had the equivalent of the Victoria Cross. He then went on to explain that for an enlisted man to earn the Military Medal three times was considered the equivalent of the Victoria Cross. Shortly after the dinner, when Fred and I were lunching one day, I proceeded to quote Ritchie's version of the Military Medal to him. He demurred, "Well, that's very kind of him, but I think not." He became so ill at ease that I felt uncomfortable for him, and his genuine embarrassment or discomfort was quite obvious. In later years when speaking of some incident that occured during the war, he would speak of "this fellow" or "one man" in relation to some heroic person, when I am very convinced by the style of the account that the tale was of himself.

Although Fred was officially bishop of the diocese as of 1 July 1955, his enthronement did not take place until St Luke's Day in October of that year. At that service, in his first pastoral address to the people of the diocese, he stressed three immediate goals: evangelism, education, and expansion. The latter, of course, was not new. Of evangelism he told his hearers that the first task of the church is the proclamation of the Gospel: "The church that has lost its sense for the cure of souls has lost its soul." Although it was to be leadership and ecumenicity for which he became best known and loved outside his own communion, yet he said nothing of this in his first address as diocesan. He did stress, however, that everything depended on education: "The day of scientific invention should give place to an age of spiritual, intellectual, and cultural creativity." Education was needed to overcome the religious illiteracy of today, which he termed "one of the biggest enemies of the Christian faith."

At the first synod session in the spring of 1956 he proposed a diocesan centre, where rooms would be available for meetings and discussions, and an auditorium for diocesan affairs. Later the same year he arranged for the purchase and enlargement of a property just north of Toronto to be used as a conference centre. Here large and well equipped facilities were to become available for the expanding efforts of the people responsible for religious education in the diocese. The next step in his program was the calling of clergy conferences in May. These conferences were part of his plan for a better informed clergy. Good planning and helpful presentations by experienced men resulted in an atmosphere of genial good will, good food, and splendid fellowship. The two or three days passed quickly, and over three hundred men returned to their parishes with a feeling they belonged to a larger church and possessed a greater awareness of their part in it. The highlight of the conference was a talk by the bishop on the role of the parson. It was a frank, friendly, and fatherly discussion ranging from the conduct of a service to relations with people both inside and out of the church. Some clergy were casual, even negligent, about their personal appearance; he would mention the importance of this in such a way that none was offended. Arthur Smith remembers these gatherings with affection: "He always had something to say that was worthwhile."

The bishop retained his concern for education; so he called his public relations people in for a meeting to which I was invited and which took place on a Saturday afternoon. He said that he wished us to explore the feasibility of a diocesan newspaper and indicated that, although he had been advised against it by lay press people, he felt it was something that we ought to do. I remember two or three meetings when we all agreed we should have a go at it. Fred announced that he would find the money and that he was appointing Dean Gilling to manage the paper; Gilling worked in the synod office as archdeacon at the time. Later Fred would appoint Kay Mathers as editor; she was to do a fine job over a period of some years. At Easter 1958 the first issue of *The Anglican* came out. It went free to every parish and was an instant success. To Walter Gilling Fred said, "Keep it going." Walter replied, "I need more money," to which the bishop responded, "That's not the problem." He requested funds for the second issue, and by the third we were solid and able to pay him back. Each paper contained a message from the bishop; some quotations from them will appear later. They were widely read and commented upon, and were admittedly of help to many people. Again in keeping with this program of education, within the year he contracted to write for the *Globe and Mail* a weekly column entitled "Canadians and Their Religion." It was here that he sowed the seed of ecumenicity. In addition to a lengthy monthly article for *The Anglican*, as well as weekly sermons for his rounds through the diocese, and addresses for state and civic functions, he tackled the new challenge of writing with dedication. He never missed a deadline.

I first came to know the bishop when I went to see him prior to my ordination to the diaconate in 1955. I was then 39, the father of five sons, and was to be entrusted with one of the new church extension parishes. Fred was coadjuter bishop with right of succession at the time and was to ordain me to the priesthood the following year when he became diocesan bishop. I found him kindly, gentle, and encouraging at our first meeting. Later, when accompanied by my architect we presented him with the sketches of the new church building, I saw a new side to him. He definitely did not like the proposed design and made plain that he would not give his approval. "Take away those things," he said, referring to the wooden flying buttresses. The things were removed, the new design approved, and the erection of St Matthias' proceeded swiftly in fields surrounded by cabbages and cauliflower.

It was a busy time; in addition to the construction a visitation program to uncover new parishioners went on by day and night. I had not seen or spoken to Fred for quite some time, but evidently he was quite familiar with our progress, for shortly before completion I received a letter from him containing a cheque with instructions to take my family away on a good holiday. This was followed later by a phone call from him to say if I did not go away for a month at least, he would not dedicate the new church. Knowing he was capable of carrying out his threat, I did as I was told. It was an example of how informed he was and how much he cared. It is a great thing to care and be concerned for others, but it is greater still to actively seek out the needy recipient. This the bishop did constantly. Leonard Hatfield, the present Bishop of Nova Scotia, recalls when he was in Toronto in a senior position with the national church, and consequently in touch with the diocesan clergy that Fred, aware of this, asked him to let him know of any situation in the life of any of his clergy or their families where his personal pastoral care was needed. Bishop Hatfield adds, "A genuine pastoral concern was there at all times, and I know from personal experience that he would move with the same incisive and generous manner into pastoral situations that he used in the administrative work of his diocese."

At the bishop's request I served on the Public Relations Committee. While I was busy building a new parish, I did not sit on committees or attend or belong to secular clubs or lodges. So I saw very little of Fred until he began to call me on the telephone to see if I would act as his chaplain at the occasional evening service out of town. I got to drive him, and he claimed he liked the way I drove; but I suspect the truth was it gave him an opportunity to rest. On our first motor trip together, as we approached the north city limits, he asked me to stop at Laura Secord, a well known candy manufacturer in Canada. He emerged clutching a box of chocolates which I thought were for our dinner host that evening. Not so, they were for himself. Surprised that I didn't want any, he proceeded to devour a fair number of them. This was my introduction to his sweet tooth which he plied with cookies and especially vanilla ice cream with chocolate sauce. On these long trips he would slouch forward on the seat, pull his hat over his eyes, and doze off for a brief nap. The nap completed, he would suggest we pull over and have a coffee. In due time we would arrive at the rectory where the good hosts had prepared a delicious meal to which the bishop and I always did justice.

Whenever he wrote sermons or articles for publication, he always had candy at hand. He was a trencherman whose favourite meal was roast beef. He never tired of it despite the vast number of times hostesses, knowing his taste, included it on the menu. Soon our journeys ceased as he was provided with a car and driver through the generosity of the well-known industrialist E.P. Taylor. Although we consequently saw less of each other, the drives together were the beginning of a friendship that we took up again after his retirement, and that flourished until his death.

LAMBETH

Every ten years bishops of the Anglican Communion gather together in what is known as the Lamberth Conference, so named because their host and chairman is the Archbishop of Canterbury whose residence in London is the Lambeth Palace. Up until 1958 only diocesan bishops attended. Fred Wilkinson appealed this successfully so that suffragans (assistant bishops) and coadjutors (right of succession) were included. Bishop Snell, the suffragan bishop of Toronto, accompanied Fred to England for the 1958 Conference. It was Fred's first visit since he had returned from Britain in 1919. Both he and Madeleine enjoyed every moment of it; he took in all the ancient and historic sites and made sure that she met many of the interesting world figures attending the conference. One of the highlights was the Queen's reception; as each bishop is presented, his name and diocese is announced. In the American church bishops do not use the term *Lord Bishop* but just *Bishop*. When one of the American bishops was called in the British fashion, "the Lord Bishop . . ." he did not come forward. After a pause the bishop's neighbour nudged him saying, "That's you." "I know," was the reply, "It sounds so lovely I want to hear it again." Fred told the story of how Bishop Bagnall, while walking in the grounds, was called over by the Archbishop of Canterbury and introduced to the Bishop of Johannesburg with the words, "I'd like you to meet the Bishop of Niagara." Johannesburg, a great huge man, looked down at Bishop Bagnall and said, "Lots of water but no diamonds." Bishop Bagnall tells how he and Fred, attired in civilian clothes, hailed a taxi. They had to wait some time for a cab, which was strange in London. Safely seated in the cab Walter mentioned this to the driver who replied, "Don't you know; this city is full of ruddy bishops from all over the ruddy world." Long afterward Fred would say to me, "Seen any ruddy Bishops lately?"

Fred was on the committee for Church Unity and Church Universal, a subject of great concern to him. Walter Bagnall says, "Fred spoke several times at the council and made a great impression. Of all there, Fred's voice stood out as one of the authentic voices that was listened to. I remember turning to my neighbour and saying, 'There's the voice of the Canadian church.' There was complete attention to him." Fred's view of Lambeth was positive if only because the concerns of other areas of the world were being heard and some honest efforts were being made to deal with them. But it also brought people together in the same way as his clergy conferences; friendships were formed and information exchanged. Being a man who naturally made many friends he lamented, "What a pity there wasn't more time," a view echoed by Richard Emrich, the retired Bishop of Michigan: "I admired Biship Wilkinson as a strong, steady, wise, and completely reliable servant of God and his church, but I admired him as it were from a distance at the Anglican Conference. And even though in Lambeth at the conference in 1958 we lived together in the same hotel for forty days, we never even had a meal together."

One of the friendships formed was with Mervin Charles-Edwards and his wife. He was then the Bishop of Worcester and met Fred at Buckingham Palace. He recounts, "After chatting for some time he offered to give us a lift. Someone had loaned him their chauffeur and Rolls Royce — an enormous thing it was — and he took us to his hotel, and we had tea with Madeleine and him, which began our friendship. He had all the marvelous qualities one admires. He had no pomp, yet he had great dignity. The first time I met him I thought, "This is a very lovable man; he exuded it'."

Indeed Fred demonstrated love in many ways. Walter Bagnall says Fred had an expression that he would use quite often. "We would talk about this or that, and finally he would say, 'Alright we've talked enough; let us do something now'. An example of this at Lambeth concerned some of the Bishops from the Third World who were lacking in robes and vestments. We had talked about it, and one day he came to me with a proposal for a few of us to chip in and buy the robes and vestments they needed, which we did. He spearheaded it; it was all done very quietly."

All too soon Lambeth came to an end but its effects remained, particularly with Fred, for immediately on his return to Toronto he addressed the Empire Club on the subject of Church unity. "This means an adventure of good will and still more of faith. Not that one communion should be absorbed by another but that we would all unite in the new and great endeavour to recover and to manifest to the world the unity of the body of Christ."

In a series of weekly letters in the fall of that year and in early 1959, the bishop reported on Lambeth and unity, and informed his people of all the details of church union schemes then in progress. He proclaimed 12 April 1959 as Ecumenical Sunday, to be observed by all churches in the diocese and preceded by prayer and study, and he requested his clergy to involve as many from other denominations as would participate. He had set up a Committee on Ecumenical Affairs in June 1957; so two year's spade work had already gone into the project. Within a year he would accept the chairmanship of an ecumenical committee for the whole of Canada, not that he needed more committees, but authority and drive was needed and the cause was closest to his heart. All his fervour for education was geared to this goal of unity; he missed no opportunity to include other heads of denominations. At a private luncheon for the visiting Archbishop of Canterbury (Ramsey), Archbishop Pocock of the Roman Catholic Church was seated on Ramsey's left, the head of the Salvation Army on his right.

Archbishop Pocock says, "This was before the days that ecumenism was really going. Fred sponsored many ecumenical affairs; he was quite a bit ahead of his time." Indeed he was; even some of his clergy looked askance at the direction he was leading them, but they were small in number and ultimately "fell in to line."

Aside from the tremendous influence that the bishop had, much of the success of the ecumenical movement in Toronto and beyond depended on the way he went about it. The program of education, in particular his written articles in the press, was crucial. But also, as Doug Mackintosh noted, "His superb sense of public relations played a great part," for he never failed to give the most serious considerations to the sensitivities of people. Reg Stackhouse approached him with the suggestion of holding his evening service in a United Church as an ecumenical gesture. Approval was readily given, but Fred added, "You had better hold a service of Evensong about 5 PM so that no person will feel deprived." Reg adds, "I thought it was a sensible gesture and a charitable one. It was a loving thing to do, not a narrow sectarian thing at all. He should have been in a larger church position because of his ecumenical outlook. He was the kind of leader the times demanded." Reg Soward agrees and adds, "I think the greatest thing about him was his ecumenicity. He was respected by all."

I remember Rabbi Gunther Plaut telling me at the time of Madeleine Wilkinson's death that it was these two people that extended the hand of friendship to him when he came to Toronto. Of the bishop he wrote, "He proved to be a man of extraordinary kindness, possessed of the broadest understanding. I always found his counsel to be wise and kindly, the mark of a true pastor rather than a clerical politician. In other words, both my wife and I have a very warm spot in our hearts for the bishop."

He esteemed Jewish people equally with Christians of any Christian denomination. He numbered among his friends Mayor Nathan Phillips, whom he once described as "a very catholic person." When the announcement of Fred's retirement was made, he was tendered a civic reception, rather a rare thing for a clergyman, since the city council was predominantly non-Anglican; Philip Gibbons was the Mayor. Gibbons, recounting the leadership and prominence of the bishop in city life, said that Wilkinson had become bishop of the city and added in the words of the popular song, "We've become accustomed to your face."

He extended the educational thrust of ecumenism by the formation in 1962 of a directorate for a Christian approach to Jewish people, the first of its kind. Under the leadership of Roland DeCorneille it functioned effectively and imaginatively for many years. In a New Year's message to his people the bishop explained about the divinely appointed feasts and observances of the Jewish people. "I like to think," he said, "of the fanfare by which the faithful were summoned to some of these feasts and the admonition, 'Blow up the trumpet in the new moon'." Once coming across a copy of a service commemorating Dominion Day in Westminster Abbey and reading the words of a hymn used on that occasion, "Trumpet of God sound high," he was inspired to write a new musical setting for it.

During the 1950s the press reported his leadership in arranging pulpit exchanges with clergy of other denominations, but it was unity he was striving for, not news. He devoutly believed in the unity of all Christians. He found the worship of others both interesting and worthwhile, and once in a discussion with Charles Dalton on this subject he remarked, "I have worshipped in every kind of Christian Church there is, and I have never had a problem if you go in the right frame of mind — to worship." It was this broad view of his that exposed narrow views and insular outlook as the first impediment to Christianity.

Dr Northrop Frye, the principal of Victoria University at the time of the honouring of Fred in Convocation in 1966, read these words about him: "He has never been doctrinally vague, but if there is more unity and understanding among Canadian Christians now than there was a generation ago, the improvement is due to his efforts." Archbishop Pocock, the retired head of the Roman Catholic Church in Toronto, illustrates this. The archdiocese had erected a magnificent new college, St Augustine, with a handsome chapel which required a suitable organ. "I turned to Fred for advice," said the archbishop. "He went out to the college and then drew up specifications and certain recommendations, which we followed! So to a large extent he is responsible for the present organ in St Augustine's College; that is one of the good things he did for me and the Church."

One marvels at the way the bishop balanced the duties of office with the things that he viewed as essential and necessary. His day would include the chairing of a meeting, a service of dedication or confirmation, an interview, attendance at a recital or concert, or some other gathering for civic or state affair. His love of music never failed; never a day went by without some bit of music being heard or played by him. Bishop Charles-Edwards commented on this when he stayed with the Wilkinson's in Toronto: "He had the most marvelous music going all day, you awakened to it in the morning; it was glorious."

He declared 1960 as Church Music Year, and in a long article traced some of the history of Church music and the importance of its place in worship, as well as the need for congregations to participate. He urged his clergy to experiment with new tunes, pointing out hymns that were theologically sound but neglected because of their hackneyed tunes. With funds bequeathed to the diocese he founded the Diocesan Choir School under the direction of Kenneth Scott and others. Musicians were drawn together in a fine spirit of co-operation and service, and gave freely of their time and talents to assist in the project. He loved to sing hymns to himself as he drove around the diocese, his words conjuring up delightful thoughts. "Driving one morning out of town the words of Newman's hymn

'Lead kindly light' came to my mind. I am often surprised at the extraordinary activity of memory which suddenly and seemingly without cause revives in one's mind events, memories, and happenings long since forgotten. Reflecting on this autobiographical hymn, unheard for a long time, as I drove through the beauty of the countryside in the light of the sun's rising rays, I felt anew the exultation and certainty of the last verse, 'So long thy power hath blest me, Sure it still will lead me on.'

It was a concern to him that the liturgical movement seemed to remove hymns that tended to identify the individual with worship. He wrote: "The very heart of our service is the words of administration: the body of our Lord Jesus Christ which was given for thee." While expressing regard for the liturgical movement and its teachings he goes on to say, "We must never forget that the corporate worship of the Church is that of countless individuals who belong to the great family of the redeemed, who have a living relationship with their living Lord." He then adds, "Only once in ten years have I heard the hymn "Jesus Lover of my Soul," and that was at a Eucharist in St Paul's Cathedral in London, England. I know there is a tendency to ostracize hymns of this kind, yet many people in their private devotions would be greatly helped if they would use hymns." It was in an effort to encourage such use that he agreed to be chairman of the joint hymnal committee of the Anglican and United Churches. He confessed that as he went about the diocese he discovered an improvement in the quality of music and, while he was delighted in the rendition of psalms and anthems, it was the singing of hymns by the people that aroused in him the real meaning of worship. He wrote in one of his articles, "Our faith and the Church are rightly and frequently referred to as being engaged in an unending warfare against evil and the powers of darkness. Christians may be accused of unrealism because of their hymns and psalm singing. What a different world we might live in if everyone knew more of the great hymns and sang them more often. What this might not do to their faith, their courage, and their morals. There is no sense in waiting until everything has been righted in this world, to sing the songs of victory. Songs of victory are meant to be sung daily and above all in the thickest of the fight."

In his music files were programs of services and recitals, including his own; annotated magazines, periodicals, and reviews, such as the *Musical Times* and the *American Organist*; and copies of letters to the authors and participants. His interest manifested itself in his attendance at concerts all over the city. I can remember later in his episcopate, occasions in my own parish when performances of Vivaldi, Schubert, Mozart, and others, were performed. Fred could be spotted in some corner of the congregation following the program from his own score.

EUROPE

In early August 1960 the Wilkinsons sailed to England on the *Empress of Britain* for what the English press referred to as a "working holiday." Free time was sandwiched in between attending World Refugee meetings in Berlin, visiting the NATO troops in Europe, and addressing the Three Choir Festival in Worcester. While in England the bishop visited the home of the Royal School of Church Music at Addington Palace to make tentative plans for a choir festival in Toronto, and paid a visit to the music publishers Novello and Company, to discuss the publishing of the revised Psalter for the Canadian Church.

He and Madeleine joined the Archbishop of York and Mrs Ramsey motoring over the Yorkshire moors, with stops at Lincoln and Norwich and two delightful days at Cambridge. They visited the Archbishop of Canterbury and Mrs Fisher at Lambeth Palace and then journeyed to Canterbury where they renewed acquaintances with Burgeon Bickersteth, former warden of Hart House in Toronto and now resident in Canterbury, who possessed an astonishing knowledge of that place and its cathedral.

They made their way north to Worcester, the site of the Three Choir Festival, and to Froxmere Court, the seat of the Bishop of Worcester, where they were to stay for the next ten days. It was a marvelous place to be, looking out on the great gardens and green meadows of England with a distant view of the cathedral and the Malvern Hills beyond. Here the bishop composed his address, given on a lovely Sunday afternoon at the opening of the festival in a most impressive ceremony. First held in 1715 the Three Choir Festival is the oldest in the World. The choirs of the medieval cathedrals of Worcester, Hereford, and Gloucester, assisted by orchestras and soloists, take turns hosting this annual event in a week of great music. There is no record unfortunately of the words Fred spoke on this occasion, but in a letter home he mentions the festival: "I have listened to such glorious works as Bach's *St Johns's Passion* and Elgar's *Dream of Gerontius* when the choirs were accompanied by the London Symphony Orchestra. I have listened to interesting modern music such as Walton's *Cello Concerto* played splendidly by a young musician from Ceylon, Rohan de Saram, *In Terra Pax* by the Swiss composer Frank Martin, the *Budavari Te Deum* of Kodaly of Hungary, who honoured the festival with his presence." He goes on to say, "One meets many interesting and delightful people at such a gathering. Real life is meeting; we need more of real Christian friendship both in the world and in the Church. How much of the misery of mankind and the spiritual impotence of the Church is due to man's callousness and the lovelessness of many professing Christians and their Church!"

At the close of the festival Fred was flown by the Royal Canadian Air Force to France and Germany where he visited with Canada's NATO forces, conducted a service of Confirmation, and preached at a Battle of Britain service. In the tranquility and beauty of the English countryside, the bishop experienced a sense of re-dedication and renewal which found its expression on his return in his enthusiasm once more for education. Earlier in 1960 a third bishop for Toronto, in the person of Harry Hunt, had been elected and consecrated. While in Edinburgh for a meeting that summer Bishop Hunt met with Fred and among other things discussed religious education in the schools. Shortly after his return Fred appointed Bishop Hunt as chairman of the education committee. Fred was disturbed by the encroachment of secularist groups on daily life. Prayer in the public schools had always been part of the curriculum. Roman Catholics attended their own schools, and Jewish parents had taken no offense at the use of the Psalms or the Lord's Prayer. But there were other groups who had set out not only in Toronto but in other parts of America to abolish all attempts at religious education in the school system where it had always been the norm. Fred's attempts to meet this threat were in general well received and certainly had some affect on the continuance of religious education.

Some months prior to this the bishop became concerned with secularism in the colleges and appointed William Bothwell, one of his clergy, to be resident chaplain at the campus of the University of Toronto, creating the first university chaplaincy in Canada. By this time he had instituted, in addition to the university chaplaincy, the Christian-Jewish Committee, the Committee on Religion in the Schools, seminars and conferences in the Diocesan Centre and the Conference Centre under the direction of the Board of Religious Education, clergy conferences, a school of music, and of course the newspaper (*The Anglican*). Always an avid reader he recommended many good books. Amid the din of battle and death in France he would take from his pocket a small book of world classics and proceed to digest the contents as if nothing else in the world mattered. After his retirement and in his later years he would often waken in the middle of the night, saunter into his study, and read. His interests were many and diverse. He urged his people to read *The Challenge of Change* by an Abbé in Belgium or a book by Oliver Wendel Holmes, or another by a professor of history in Natal University in South Africa. Reg Stackhouse says, "He never lost his academic interest in spite of his constant round of activity; he was a reader of serious theological works. Up until a week before he died he would put me to shame by saying, 'Have you read such and such?' It was always one of the latest." Often when he felt some book would be beneficial to his clergy, he would order several hundred and send one to each of them with his compliments. Indeed this was a favourite method of his to advocate some cause, for example, his native land: "He had a great feeling for the history of Canada and would send us books about it. The last one was *Six Great Lives*," says Lord Nugent.

The books in his extensive library, particularly theological books, would often be marked with neat comments in his handwriting in the margin. Something in a book would sometimes suggest some line of action to one of his committees as a way of assisting in this or that program. Authors would occasionally receive letters praising their work or gently disagreeing with some line they had taken or were promoting. In many of his addresses and sermons he introduced quotations not only to emphasize a point but also to share with the listener certain passages of great literature. In later years he indulged in detective stories and science fiction, but continued to read spiritual and theological writings as well as the biographical works. He would discourse in the most animated way about something he had read. I remember his telling about *The Sinking of the Tirpitz*, and finding it difficult to believe he had not been involved.

Earlier mention has been made of the bishop's concern for his clergy. He arranged conferences and meetings to bring them together, visitations, lunches, and dinners. But there were also occasions when financial assistance was needed. Through his business and political associations he sought to contact those in a position to help. The result was the Bishop's

Men, a dedicated group of financial contributors. These men, two hundred of them the first year, established a contingency fund for use by the bishop, who would meet with them once a year over dinner and report to them on the disposition of the funds. Some eighty benefactions one year included assistance to the Diocesan Choir School to allow more boys to attend at a reduced fee, providing a chaplain for the police courts, a grant for special ministry to the Eskimo at the Weston Sanitarium, assistance to retired and elderly clergy living on small pensions, enabling a priest to visit his father who was dying in England, a grant to clergy whose children had extended bouts of illness, and grants to widows of clergy. Budgetary problems of several clergy were happily resolved: "I have insisted that a number of clergy take their wives and themselves on a holiday — grants for same."

The special needs which always exist, and for which regular provisions do not exist, were met on a scale which the bishop's contingency fund could not cover. In his letters he was always careful to mention that a gift came from "funds made available to me." Everyone who knew him marvelled at his extraordinary kindness, expressed not only in money but in time also. "The kindest man I ever knew," was Harry Price's description of him, a view echoed by Bishop Snell: "He was always very kind, considerate, and generous. He gave a great dinner in my honour at the Royal York; hundreds were there. He didn't have to do that; he was great at that sort of thing. On another occasion in 1947, when it was announced that I was going to Calgary, he called me up to say he wanted me to have lunch with him. He was then at St Paul's and just recovering from an operation. He still wasn't very peppy, but he wanted to have a chat with me about Calgary and tell me what he knew about things there. I was a complete stranger to him, and yet out of the blue he did this for me."

He agreed to one of his clergy going to Yale for further studies, saying that he would support him. Accompanying each cheque was a letter of interest and encouragement. "He was like a gentle father with his clergy, all the more impressive because he was such a strong man. He could have been the opposite, just domineering, but he was dominant in the right sense." There was no doubt that some took advantage of his kindness. One of his senior administrators of those days remarked, "He would make appointments for kindly reasons, to leg a man up. He was kind to a fault in that sense." In the words of Reg Stackhouse, "His money went to helping people in need, in helping causes, and in being open handed with his clergy. He was very soft about money."

George Snell says, "I think his administrative ability was demonstrated more in the kind of people he chose to do jobs. That's where he was good. He would go into the office of the president of the Bank of Montreal or some other leading institution; the first thing you knew that guy would be contributing his talents. That was Fred's great strength." He would pick up the phone and reach the top men in every field of human endeavour. The Honourable John Aird says, "If you ask me who of all the people I have met in the Church who commanded more respect from more people and who had the largest constituency of friends, I would say Fred Wilkinson." His curates had great admiration for his organizing ability. Richard Newsham admired this gift: "At St Pauls we had the top men in industry, medicine, and law. Fred had them organized and committed, and these men were all close personal friends of his. They were the sheep following the shepherd. When he was bishop he surrounded himself with men (clergy and laity) in the same way. You could always get an answer and action, and you could always get to him in person without any nonsense."

The wife of an out of town clergyman came to see him one day; her husband's pay had been discontinued during his operation and convalescence. Fred was appalled. Cancelling his appointments he left the office and drove the lady the long journey home outside the city, visited with the couple, interviewed the two wardens of the parish and told them in no uncertain terms that they would pay the man's salary in full and, in addition, his medical expenses. If they did not carry this out he would dis-establish the parish! Lexi Mackintosh recalls with fondness the way in which he came to her after the death of her first husband, the Rev John Riddell, to assure her that he would make up the difference between her pension and her husband's salary until she found suitable employment, however long it might take.

Every man of course has his detractors, and the bishop was no exception. There were those who thought him tough, for example, concerning his observance of the Sabbath. This stand is not surprising in view of his own childhood when Evangelical and Victorian views were enforced. In his later years he began to enjoy a glass of wine or a cocktail with dinner. He also took to smoking a pipe or an occasional cigarette. But perhaps it was a good cigar he enjoyed most, particularly after dinner. "It is just an impression," says Archbishop Pocock, "but I felt he mellowed latterly."

ANGLICAN CONGRESS

In 1954 in Minneapolis the bishop issued an invitation for an Anglican Congress in 1963; so for almost ten years the thoughts and plans of the Church were directed to this congress, and the slogan "Toronto in '63" became familiar throughout the churches of the Anglican Communion.

According to protocol an invitation had first to be approved by the diocesan synod and then forwarded for approval to the General Synod of the Church of Canada. From here it went to the Primate of all Canada, and with his approval was forwarded to the Archbishop of Canterbury, who in turn issued the invitation to all dioceses of the Anglican Communion. The conference was to run from 13 to 23 August 1963. Each diocese was to send it's bishop, one priest, and one layman as official delegates. In addition all coadjuter and suffragan bishops were invited as well as selected youth delegates. In addition to the 1200 delegates would be wives, members of the press, and observers from other denominations. Many more, particularly from the United States and Canada, would attend in order to witness the proceedings, especially the two services to be held in Maple Leaf Gardens. The planning for such an event was both vast and detailed, and the theme "the Church's Mission to the World" was immense in its implications.

The success of the congress was built on a superb team of organizers who worked over a long period of time with unselfish dedication and goodwill. From the moment the invitation was accepted the bishop proceeded to set the stage. He decided on the key figures and then went after them. In January 1961 he announced the first three of these: the Right Honourable Vincent Massey, former Governor General of Canada, as patron; R.C. Birkinshaw, the Toronto industrialist, as honorary chairman; and Colonal J.C.K. Strathy, Toronto financier, as Chairman. Reg Soward says, "When I think of the congress, Fred had the ability to pick the right people, and then he left them to do it. He didn't interfere with them so long as they followed the lines he laid down." To chair the several committees he carefully chose some people who were tops in their field. One of these, Mrs Pat MacKay, remembers receiving a call from the bishop inviting her to lunch at the York Club. "When it was over I found myself chairman of the ladies committee." It was this committee that was responsible for the daily breakfasts in the Diocesan Centre; some 1000 breakfasts had to be prepared every morning. The committee was also responsible for the tea tents on the campus of the University of Toronto and for two large dinners in private homes during the congress. "Fred tried to develop his strength to work with committees, to inspire people to do more than they thought they could. He was never angry, but always congenial, placid, in control." Harry Wilson, an executive committee member, echos this: "On committee work Fred was always alert to suggestion; he listened. He never wasted time — which businessmen appreciated. He was a wonderful chairman; he had a tidy mind and followed through." General Legge was heavily involved with the transportation committee for the congress, and he speaks of the meetings at which Fred was present. "He was a no-nonsense chairman and kept the agenda moving. The atmosphere was formal — 'my Lord' throughout — but with a good feeling. He was a warm imposing man, two hundred per cent a bishop, a big man. He fronted the congress, he was the figure, and that's magnificent when the general comes on the field."

In addition to setting up the committees Fred made advance arrangements for space. A central location was needed for all the plenary sessions and social gatherings. The Canadian Pacific Railway generously provided the extensive facilities of the Royal York Hotel. Fred negotiated with the University of Toronto for the use of their buildings and grounds. He was concerned that the delegates should not be prevented from attending the congress through lack of funds, and in many instances he arranged for travel expenses. Living accommodations and meals in private homes were also provided. St Michael's Roman Catholic School hosted a choir, and off duty firemen acted as drivers. Every delegate was met on arrival, transported to and fro, and taken to the airport or railway station at the end of the congress. One delegate, a member of the Parliament of Nigeria, expressed a desire to see Canada's capital. In no time, through the good offices of General Legge, he was on a flight to Ottawa with a note to the Honourable Paul Hellyer, then minister of National Defense. An officer and car were put at his disposal so that he could view government installations in Ottawa. A delighted Mr Akomalafe returned to Toronto amazed at the services provided.

The Archbishop of Canterbury's hand woven flag mysteriously disappeared from the front fender of his car at the very opening of the congress, and despite coverage in the press it never turned up. It was obviously in the custody of some souvenir hunter. The driver of the car, a devout Roman Catholic, was named by his fellow firemen as the culprit in a neferious plot to send the flag to Rome as a trophy! In the early stages of the preparations for the congress it was suggested that the event should be held in Japan in order to give the Church in Japan strength. Fred consulted with Archbishop Yashiro, head of the Japanese Church who, however, said it would be absolutely impossible for their Church to act as host at that time, and insisted most emphatically that plans for the Toronto congress must go ahead. At this stage Fred sent Bishop Snell to visit with the Church in Ireland, Wales, and Scotland while he himself met with York and Canterbury. Then on his return he went to the United States to consult with the presiding bishop of the Church there. Meanwhile the many committees involved met with increasing regularity to discuss agendas, ticketing, billeting, catering, worship, press, radio, and TV coverage. Expenses were to be borne by the Canadian Church through special contributions, the Toronto Diocese being the major contributor. Bishop Bagnall of Niagara was in charge of finance.

In committee Fred was indefatigable — at times officiating, in most cases listening and offering helpful suggestions. As mentioned earlier he had the gift of appointing people and leaving them to do the job. When he learned the Archbishop of Canterbury was being taken out of town by one of the Canadian bishops for some local function in his own diocese, Fred quietly made plain the impossibility of Canterbury's absence from any congress function and the excursion was stopped.

The opening of the congress took place in the huge Canadian Room of the Royal York Hotel attended by delegates, representatives of the three levels of government, official observers from other Churches, and members of the public media. Fred as host bishop followed the Archbishop of Canterbury to the lectern, welcomed the delegates, and stressed the need for an adventurous spirit and a sense of direction in their deliberations. The congress was for him the logical step to be taken by

the Anglican Church, an ever widening process of self education and evaluation. In the official report *Anglican Congress
1963*, the eminent Canadian theologian Eugene Fairweather
writes about those attending: "In their minds the mention of
Toronto will evoke memories of stirring challenges sounded
and accepted, of new duties faced and acknowledged, of hard
questions put and strange paths explored. For them Toronto
will be the place where they heard the call to a new reformation
of the Anglican community."

The congress was a great triumph for Fred because it
brought so many people together in a wonderful spirit of goodwill. The arrival of the three metropolitan archbishops of the
Orthodox Church to present a cross to the Archbishop of
Canterbury from the Metropolitan of Constantinople was a
visibly moving moment. James Cardinal McGuigan, Archbishop Pocock, and Paul-Emile Cardinal Leger had asked that
prayers for the Anglican Congress be offered in every church
in their dioceses. Other denominations followed suit. The
great opening service was a memorable event. Diocese by
diocese the delegates processed down Church Street to Carlton
Street, bishop and priest fully robed, lay delegates often in
colourful native dress. Inside the arena they were greeted by
thousands singing the processional hymns. Going before them
was a server carrying a banner with the names: the Church of
Wales; the Church of Ireland; the Episcopal Church of
Scotland; the Episcopal Church in the United States; the
Church of India, Pakistan, Burma, and Ceylon; the Church of
England in Australia and Tasmania; the Church of New
Zealand; the Church of South Africa; the Church of the West
Indies; Nippon Sei Ko Kai of Japan; the Churches of West
Africa, Central Africa, East Africa; and then Uganda and
Rwanda and Burundi; and many more.

In his address that evening the Archbishop of Canterbury
said, "Towards other Churches we work for unity in truth and
holiness . . . as to the goal, it is nothing less than full communion in and of the Catholic Church of Christ. In the process

part of the Anglican family may cease to be precisely Anglican as United Churches come into being in full communion with us." This statement set the tone for the congress and it made a deep and lasting impression.

The bishop believed that the congress had achieved what he had hoped for, that it had brought the entire Anglican Communion into a position where it was ready seriously to enter into union negotiations with other bodies. Reg Stackhouse in speaking of this aspect of Fred's career says, "He conceived the congress, he prepared for it, he organized it, he undertook financial obligations without which it could not have been held, and I don't know if he ever received the recognition for it. He never took the centre of the stage; the only time he took any position in connection with it was at the great opening service when he walked in procession as the host bishop. He constantly was self effacing when another man quite properly would have claimed some of the limelight. He arranged for others to occupy positions while he sat in the shadows having made it all happen, which is some indication of his own spirituality." Senator Walker observes, "From all sources you hear that the congress was a magnificent achievement. Even in England they said it was unprecedented. It was extremely well organized, and Fred himself was responsible for it." Mervyn Charles-Edwards the bishop of Worcester affirms this: "The congress was of great value for us in the United Kingdom; in fact it gave us a marvellous insight into the people of other countries, South Africa for instance. It certainly had a positive effect on our later discussion on Church union with the Methodists." This was also the view of Lord Coggan who attended as Archbishop of York: "The effects of the congress were to be felt in the years ahead, as we were made aware of the needs and problems of others around the world and were moved to contribute both money and manpower. Some denominations became more open in their approach to others,

notably the Roman Catholic Church, and some began discuss-
ing union, particularly between our own church and the
Methodists in Britain."

Mrs Charles-Edwards felt that Fred's guiding influence was
significant. "He was incredible. It was marvellous the way
everyone was included and could attend deliberations and
addresses. For wives of the delegates, this was quite new. It
was another part of Fred's genius; all were included as
members of the Church." Lord Ramsey, then Archbishop of
Canterbury, remembers the congress as a real success. "It
brought together the very different elements in the Anglican
communion and the Christian fellowship, with the give and
take of final discourse. Thanks to Bishop Wilkinson's share
and the planning, everything went effortlessly without any
fuss or confusion; so much had been done quickly behind the
scenes. We realize that we owe very much to him for the entire
success of the congress."

What thoughts must have been in Fred Wilkinson's mind on
the night of the opening service, as in the very vicinity of his
early home, he walked at the end of a great procession of
dignitaries from around the world! He had come a long way in
fulfilling the vow he made in Flanders in 1917 to "take up the
torch" in the cause of his brother Harold. Those close to him
agree that he viewed the congress and its results with the
greatest of happiness.

THE 1960'S

In the wake of war there seems always to follow a period of
cynicism when everything of value is scrutinized and somehow made responsible for past wrongs and present miseries.
After World War II an increasing number felt the Church to be
fair game; in every corner of the world religion was under
attack. Churches became the scene for protest of all kinds.

Clergy were ridiculed and the ancient dogmas and doctrines laughed at. No branch of the Christian Church was exempt. "God is dead" became the well known slogan and the subject of hotly contested debates, marches, and sit-ins. Fred remained strong in defense of the faith, and his own clergy remained stolid. He regarded the "current over publicized cult as having too many indications of exhibitionism to be taken seriously. I am not much impressed by the pseudo-theologians of today. I think the Church today should discourage the current spectacles of exhibitionism through public doubts. I cannot imagine any 'God is dead' cult emanating from the theologians of Scotland to whom the whole Christian Church owes so much."

On the eve of Holy Week one year, the Canadian Broadcasting Corporation aired a parody of the crucifixion, in which a motorcycle gang played a leading part. Fred was outraged and did his best to stop it, firing off a telegram to the head of the Canadian Broadcasting Corporation: "Such a presentation could only be sacreligious, unhistorical, and offensive to all Christians." The press entered the fray with glee and Fred's objections only served to give publicity to the program. It was an instance, however, of his defence of principles against the growing secularism that was beginning to be such a force in the city. He warned that the undermining of religion would result in the lowering of ethical and moral standards: "The blatancy with which novelists, playwrights, and film producers degrade sex, ridicule wholesome standards of morality, and extol what is vicious and degrading, can only result in the moral decay of our society and in innumerable human tragedies." He foresaw the increase in violence, the break up of the family unit, and the frequency of common-law marriages, and he continued to write and speak with intensity in defense of the traditional faith.

"People need vision," he wrote, "They need to feel there is an ideal city state, to realize there is a city of God as well as a city of man." Speaking before a great flower festival in St Louis,

With the Hon George Drew and the Hon Earl Rowe, Lieutenant-Governor of Ontario.

At Lambeth Palace with Michael Ramsey, Archbishop of Canterbury.

Reviewing the Guard of Honour of NATO Troops in Europe.

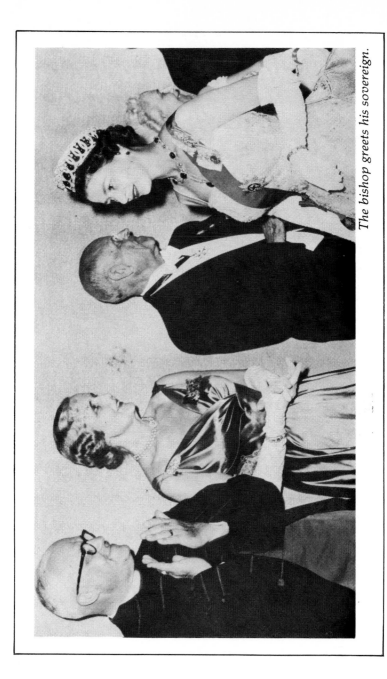

The bishop greets his sovereign.

The bishop with his son-in-law, John Hoolihan, and the author at St Anne's, Easter day, 1980.

At retirement dinner, Royal York Hotel.

Missouri, he said, "Any form of true beauty in this world is but a forerunner of the beauty which is everlasting. We live in this world not merely to cultivate our own pleasant surrounding but to share the divine task of helping to make this world a garden rather than a desert."

He continued to write a weekly article for the *Globe and Mail* and a monthly article for the *Anglican*, both were widely read and quoted. In one article on the qualities of life he wrote, "I believe God looks benevolently upon the courageous," to which he added a portion of his address in St Louis: "A young soldier was asked what was the great thing he had seen on the battle field in World War I. His reply was 'In one of our attacks near Vimy Ridge I was advancing with the fourth wave of infantry. For some reason I happened to keep my eye fixed on the man immediately in front of me some 200 yards or so ahead. As we moved forward a shell burst near him and a great cloud of smoke obscured him from my view. As the air cleared, to my amazement, I saw he was kneeling on one knee. Suddenly he picked up his rifle, slung it over his shoulder, and ran forward to catch up with his comrades. I lost sight of him as he disappeared in the smoke and the din of battle. When I came up to the place where he had stopped, to my astonishment I saw that he had taken time to replant a solitary poppy that had survived the explosion of the shell.' Such was the triumph of the human spirit in the face of death and destruction."

Another interest for Bishop Wilkinson was the plight of senior citizens and housing for them. He set up a committee and appealed to churches and people to come forward with ideas, land, and money for housing facilities. When I went to him with a proposal to transfer my church rectory and land into a separate corporation to finance one of these projects, this unprecedented step received his instant approval. He addressed an appeal to his clergy for increased interest to the Orthodox Churches, recommending reading on the subject and assuming the presidency of the order of St Alban and St Sergius, an Anglican organization for furthering relations with the Orthodox Church.

In the bishop's charge to the diocese on 1 June 1965 Fred stressed Church unity. This address was followed by an ecumenical service in the Cathedral and later a service of prayer and witness in St Paul's where the preacher was Archbishop Pocock of the Roman Catholic Church. The presence of members of other denominations at services is now the accepted thing, but this was not the case before the time of Fred Wilkinson. He was indeed the first ecumenist of the Canadian Church. Not only did he go out of his way to include others in Christian worship; on every occasion possible he was present at worship in other denominational Churches, vested and willing to participate. He appeared at Berkley Divinity School of Yale University to be awarded an honorary degree, presented with these words: "Frederick Hugh Wilkinson, Bishop of Toronto, who after deserving well of the Anglican Church of Canada in many offices, as Professor of Theology, parish priest, canon, and dean, now in the order of the episcopate, labours devotedly for the good estate of the Holy Catholic Church, not only in his own fatherland but throughout the world." It was at this time that he agreed to serve on the Committee of Ten on Church union between the Anglican and the United Church. At the same time he became chairman of the Joint Hymnal Committee of the Anglican and United Church.

Indefatigable worker that he was, the bishop knew how to relax, and from time to time he would arrange a week or two for Madeleine and himself to get away. He loved to visit historic sites; I remember one post-Easter week when I took my wife and sons on a trip to Virginia. We arrived in time on Sunday for the early service at Bruton parish Church in Williamsburg, only to find the Bishop of Toronto and his wife in the pew opposite. In typical fashion nothing would do but that we should accompany them to their hotel for breakfast; there were seven of us.

Their favorite resort, however, was in Maine where they visited often over the years; here he would walk by the sea which he loved and renew acquaintances. Laman Bruner was one of these; he lived in the lighthouse at Castine, and it was here that the Wilkinsons often visited with the large Bruner family. Nearby lived Bishop William Scarlett of Missouri. Laman remembers "how exciting it was for me to hear those two great stalwarts talk and exchange stories and experiences." On one occasion Eleanor Roosevelt arrived for a delightful visit and engaged in animated discussion with the two bishops and Laman. She believed in religious education in the schools, and was thus in good company. Of the discussion Laman says, "They believed that education in the faith and subject matter could turn the world around and create new visions of kindness amongst and towards all people," a familiar theme for the Bishop of Toronto. Laman adds, "Fred was dedicated to the furthering of friendship between Canada and the United States, which he believed would come in many ways, but especially through the Church." It was to this end he encouraged clergy exchanges as well as episcopal gatherings.

At the 1965 session of the synod of the diocese on 1 June, Fred announced that he would retire on 30 June of the following year. It was an announcement that came as a shock because he could have stayed in office for another three years. Certainly no one wanted him to go, and the feeling was one of great regret. He trusted that the one thousand delegates present would not think that he planned retirement "from the battle of Christian life or the warfare of the Church Militant." Then, obliquely referring to uninformed comments in a local newspaper, he rehearsed his own beliefs and efforts concerning Church unity. His voice ringing out, he said, "I have spoken, I have written, I have prayed, I have worked and acted in private and in public, to forward and demonstrate the unity of the Church in fulfillment of our Lord's own prayer 'that they may all be one that the world may believe', and so I shall continue to work and pray until the end of my life." It was

an emotional moment, and with a spontaneous standing ovation, all rose to salute him. "I hope, said he, to have some years
free from the pressure of official duties when I may yet be of
some help to my brother clergy and laity," a wish which was to
be richly fulfilled.

From the time of the announcement until his retirement the
following year, his days were spent making farewells to the
clergy and people of the diocese as well as organizations,
groups, and corporations within the city and the province of
Ontario. He told the press that he was planning to retire to a
diet of reading, Beethoven, and golf. Golf was one of his long-
standing delights, which he often recommended to his clergy
as a wonderful way of getting out into the open. Apparently
his game was average; comments from his golfing companions
range from "Not worth a damn" to the more charitable
"Steady." But Senator Walker says, "He just loved to be out
with the boys," and his love of the game was evidenced by the
way he tried to interest others in it. He was, of course, made
welcome at all the clubs but most often played at the Hunt
Club, where some of the young members once purloined one
of his socks which became a trophy in a ski race. Walker
remembers Fred at the Hunt Club: "He had a way of drawing
men to him; he was highly regarded. He had all sorts of friends
who would delight to go around the course with him."

At a dinner to honour the then Prime Minister of Canada,
the Honourable John Diefenbaker, the head table guests were
in an anti-room prior to the dinner when Mr Diefenbaker spotted the bishop decked out in his formals complete with medals.
Mr Diefenbaker, himself a veteran of World War I, instantly
spotted the Military Medal with bars on Fred's chest and
became visably excited, calling others over. Bishop Snell
remembers that the head table party was delayed entering the
main hall for dinner. "Never saw anything like it" or "this must
be the only one in Canada," he said and wanted to know from
Fred how he earned them. The one encounter that Fred himself
liked to tell concerns Field Marshall Montgomery who was in

Toronto on a ceremonial occasion. Fred apparently was not wearing decorations or "Monty" would not have asked the question that he did. "Now then bishop, what rank did you hold?" and to Monty's chagrin Fred replied, "Lance Corporal Sir." Bob Dann says, "It was astonishing how many men there were who wanted to help out when Fred was retiring, both within and beyond the Anglican Church." To Lloyd Richardson he was "a knight of old like the knights of Malta and yet very much a Renaissance man." "I would think," says Senator Walker, "that the same courage which he showed when indignant was what stood him during the war. He would stand no nonsense if it came to a showdown. On the other hand, he wasn't prissy or narrow minded. He believed in good manners and good ethics, and he stood up for them."

He also was busy this last year looking for a place to live, for of course, on retirement the family would have to leave their official residence. If ever anyone could be said to live by faith it was Fred. By his dress, manner, and style of living he exuded affluence when in fact he most often had little or no money. When on active service in Flanders he cabled home at least twice for money to go on leave. In France his wants were modest by every standard, and in later life he occupied positions which paid well at the time. Yet in order to take the family away on holidays he borrowed on his insurance, and at the time of his retirement he could only consider renting, not owning, a home. Here was a man who raised millions for his Church and who supervised or at least administered the disposition of the same yet was truly a poor clergyman. As put by one of his senior clergy, "He had an ability that is essential to good administration: he never had any money; he never had any interest in money other than to spend it." Reg Soward admits, "He thought big; he always did. But financially he was terrible as far as his personal affairs went. He wasn't interested in private investments."

Fred's greatest investment was in life and the lives of people. He bought things to give pleasure — books, records — but very often he gave them away as donations to causes or to parishes which he visited. When it became known that he was looking for a house to rent, a quiet turmoil arose. Some leading laymen looked into the situation and discovered that Fred was retiring on some $6,300.00 a year and that he certainly was in no position to raise a down payment for a house. One of these laymen, Harry Wilson, quietly made some phone calls, and in no time the money was raised to purchase a lovely home in north Toronto for the sole use of the bishop and Mrs Wilkinson, the same to be kept up by the diocese into whose possession it would finally come. "It was the easiest money I have ever raised," said Harry Wilson.

Fred Wilkinson knew many men of influence, and he was continually challenging them. Bob Dann describes his relationship with these people: "If he went after the wealthy he went after them for the glory of God and not to line his own pocket. He never took a cent from any of them; he gave them far more than they gave him: he gave them a new dimension." His sister Jean said, "He never asked anything or took anything for himself." Reg Stackhouse comments, "When he retired he wouldn't have had a roof over his head if it hadn't been for the men who admired him so much, which is another indication of his greatness."

Archbishop Pocock smilingly remembers asking Fred what was the first thing he was going to do when he retired. "Read the Bible through from cover to cover," replied Fred. The Archbishop asked, "Which version?" to which Fred replied, "The King James of course!" The life and honorary memberships with honours and awards poured in along with gifts of money, silver, and other expressions of esteem and appreciation. On 30 June he left his office for the last time and went with Madeleine to their new home, bringing to an end forty-two years in the active ministry.

OUT OF OFFICE

For Fred Wilkinson, as for many others, retirement was only nominal. This new phase of his life was not a withdrawal; with administrative duties over he now had additional time to begin a larger and more personal ministry. Every cleric will agree to the large amount of time taken up by the demands of office. He must oversee fund raising, parish administration, property management, building, committees, and other activities that steal precious time from his main role as pastor. A bishop in addition must attend confirmation, ordination, induction, and other official functions that tend to remove him from personal contact with his people. During his days as diocesan bishop, Fred, as we have seen, had sought to overcome this by clergy conferences, receptions at his home, and more particularly by luncheons and dinners. These he now expanded to include laity as well as clergy. Hardly a day would go by but a meeting would be arranged for one or two at Simpsons, Eatons, the York Club, or some other club, and while good food played an important part, it was not the sole reason for gathering together. Conversation was spirited, questions were asked, ideas were shared.

An early riser Fred would begin the day with prayers, a series of physical exercises, and a good breakfast. This was followed by a review of the paper, which too often carried a familiar name in the obituary column. A notation was made to visit the next of kin later in the day. After reading the paper his telephoning would begin — a thank you to the previous day's host or hostess, or an invitation for future dates. On many occasions I picked up the phone to hear the bishop's cheery voice asking me to meet him for lunch or to provide some information he thought I might have. I would try to converse in as bright a manner as possible to conceal the fact that I was still in bed!

There was nothing aimless about his day; visits, calls, and appointments were scheduled and maintained. If time permitted, a late afternoon nap would help to prepare for the evening program. He would often attend functions when an important person was being honoured, and his presence was regarded with much pleasure. The word would go around, "Bishop Wilkinson is here," and at the close of the ceremony people would gravitate to him. A friend of musicians he tried to attend many recitals and concerts where, as an artist of repute, his comments were welcomed. One Sunday he dropped in for morning service at a well known non-Anglican Church. Although attired in collar and tie he was recognized, and toward the close of the service the minister announced the presence of the bishop, requesting that he give his blessing to the congregation. Later Fred spoke warmly of this gracious gesture as evidence of the gospel at work.

In the summer of his retirement year after a holiday in Maine, he delivered addresses in Albany, Calgary, Montreal, and New York. He was also at the same time chairman of the Joint Hymnal Committee of the Anglican and United Churches, a committee which was beginning to consume a great deal of his time. It was a difficult task they faced, and at times some of the committee were also difficult. Customary values were considered old-fashioned by some, and hymns of meaning and comfort to many were ruled out. " Onward Christian soldiers" was discarded but then quickly reinstated in response to the indignation of many people. Some of the evening hymns were ommitted, along with several of Fred's favourites, including the navy hymn "Eternal Father strong to save." William Kilbourn says, "I was put on the committee by Fred to save the war hymns," referring to the two already mentioned and several others. "I was impressed at the way he could remain objective with those like myself who are more leftist then he, or a certain clergyman whom he liked but who was of a controversial nature, or again those of high-church leanings like myself and therefore critical of the theology of certain hymns, yet it never interfered with his decisions or his objectivity." The hymnal was adopted in February 1971 and met with mixed reviews. It was a handsome book, beautifully designed but many of the favourite hymns had gone. Some argued that the hymns that were left out had no appeal for the young people; however, high school and university students invariably asked for the old familiar hymns. Fred helped to introduce the book to the church with addresses and musical performances, and in no small measure that its acceptance is owing to him.

In the summer of 1967 the bishop and his wife visited England, Ireland, and France, during May and June. Fred took Madeleine on a tour of the battle fields and the war cemetaries, noting the names of comrades of fifty years before. It was a year now since retirement, and he was enjoying every moment of the new life, doing the things he had always done but having much more time for them. William Kilbourn speaks of seeing Fred at a public function or gathering: "When I would see the bishop, I always made for him; he was easily the most interesting person there." He was now in his seventies and out of office, yet regardless of what official or dignitary was present on such occasions he tended to be the dominent figure in the room. Scarce two years had passed since leaving office, yet seeing him in action at meetings or affairs it was difficult to believe he was retired. His daughter Joan says, "In retirement Mother and Father were very active, attending functions, giving dinner parties, and when possible they would babysit our two children Kathy and John. They were great grandparents.

Shortly after retirement he accepted the offer of the province of Ontario to become the chairman of the Central Review Board, a position arranged through the offices of Harry Price. By law anyone committed to an institution for mental disorder was entitled to a hearing before the Review Board within thirty days. There were five members on the board including representatives of the medical and legal professions. Fred enjoyed the new challenge. Price says, "He was great." Ken Jarvis, one of the committee, describes him: "He was very much an innerdirected man; by that I mean he had within him a scale of rightness and propriety. He was one of those who would say, 'It may work; it is attractive, even practical; but it's wrong, and for that reason we can't do it'." Some of the hearings took place in Toronto and vicinity, although the majority were held in Penetang where the criminally insane were incarcerated. Ken Jarvis drove Fred the considerable distance on these trips. He remembers how Fred would come out of the house in the early morning, full of good spirits, and would chat and reminisce for most of the journey. Later he would ask permission for a snooze: "You don't mind if I just close my eyes?"

During interviews patients considered dangerous would have soft cuffs on their hands and ankles. Fred didn't like to put anyone at a disadvantage, and preferred to see the patients treated normally. "He felt it was preferable to the dignity of the man appearing before him," says Jarvis. "One man — paranoic, schizophrenic, extremely violent, husky, tall, well built, and as strong as an ox — appeared in a small room, and although the staff were very much concerned, Fred had the cuffs taken off. "Tell him to sit down; we're not worried," said Fred. "The man sat there in deep smouldering hatred, tense and coiled. Fred was calm and conciliatory to him, as usual able to meet people like that with an evident knowledge of the world. Whenever he spoke to you, you knew Fred Wilkinson knew what was what. There was no blarney or unnecessary soft

sympathy, but a firm, kindly, warm appreciation of the diffi-
culties, even to men of that ilk. It was an approach that was not
lost even to the sickest patient."

To Fred's surprise I once appeared before him on behalf of a
lady who had been committed to an institution, although she
was not a danger either to herself or others. Watching him in
this new role, as he questioned medical opinion, the patient,
and myself, I had the impression of a knowledgeable man of
great and long experience at his job. His command of the hearing was gentle, sympathetic, and understanding. He retained
this position with the board until in 1976 when he resigned at
the age of eighty.

One of the founders of CARE Canada, Ken Andras, speaks
of the wise, helpful, and friendly assistance Fred gave to CARE
when it was founded in 1956. He joined the executive committee when still bishop of Toronto and remained on during
retirement. Mr Andras says, "He had a great feeling and concern for people less fortunate both in Canada and beyond. He
was always helpful and extremely supportive."

In April 1968 he hosted the meeting of the Anglican World
Fellowship of Prayer in Toronto; he was the international
chairman. Over the years this fellowship had made its mark in
the life of the Anglican Church in many ways. Its members
compiled and published a daily cycle of prayer covering every
corner of the world Anglican Communion, bringing to light
the names of people and places all around the globe.

Although the joint hymnal was adopted by the Anglican
and United Churches the proposed merger of the two churches
failed. Fred had been a member of the committee on union and
had voted with other members to adopt the statement of prin-
cipals adding, "I intend to give this scheme my fullest support
in every possible way." He held a press conference which was
reported in the newspapers on 22 March 1969 under the
heading "Bishop offers a solution." Calling him a senior states-

man who thinks he has the solution to what promises to be the toughest problem to union, it says that "he sees the Act of Unification proposed . . . as involving a reciprocal laying on of hands." In Bishop Wilkinson's view the act would involve Anglican clergy — bishops, priests, and deacons — kneeling before United Church representatives, who would place their hands on the head of each cleric in a ritual that is part of the ordination in both churches. At the same service there would be a similar laying on of hands for United Church clergy by the Anglican bishops. Noting the apprehension in the matter of unifying ministries, he said the resolution of this problem would take "the greatest humility and forbearance and a willingness to give up certain temporal benefits for the greater blessing of the United Church. I am quite prepared to kneel and have United Church Presbyters lay hands on me in the same way I would lay hands on them." He further added that "success of the proposal for an act of unification should demand the absence of pride or a calling in question of the validity of one another's ministries." Then Bishop Wilkinson suggested the acts should be considered simply "by the grace of God extending to one another our ministries." No man either in Canada or Britain had at that time given greater lead to the cause of unification than Fred Wilkinson. Charles Dalton, a leading layman in Toronto and a proponent of union feels that the failure bothered Fred more than anything else.

"Bishop Wilkinson," said the *Globe and Mail*, "argued the continued existence of the so called "high and low" church forces in the Anglican church should be a source of reassurance to those who fear organic union would lead to uniformity." It would be a grave error to tell of his life and omit mention of this important aspect of it. He was of course a very low churchman in thought and practice, and in his funeral arrangements he is careful to point out his opposition to a cope and mitre, writing "I cannot separate myself from the old traditions of my predecessors, including my beloved father and all his generation." From its inception the diocese had always observed a middle of the road or "broad church" type of service similar to that of Westminister Abbey or St Paul's in London.

There were a number of parishes of Evangelical background in the diocese and a similar number of Anglo-Catholic background, these traditions being always scrupulously observed in the appointing of new rectors, for to appoint one to "raise" or to "lower" the churchmanship of a parish was inevitably to invite trouble. Fred was always respectful and careful not to injure the feelings or sensitivities of church people, visiting all parishes equally and honouring clergy and laity without regard for churchmanship. Bishop Charles-Edwards, retired Bishop of Worcester, commenting on Fred's handling of issues of churchmanship says, "Well, you see, with a man like Fred, that kind of nonsense breaks down." Once he and I had lunch with Bishop Snell in the King Edward hotel in Toronto, Fred being in his jovial mood and about to retire, Bishop Snell succeeding him. With a twinkle in his eye he remarked, 'I've been toying with the idea of wearing cope and mitre at my last service!' Bishop Snell caught the meaning instantly, that he would be expected to carry on the custom, the two of them dissolving in laughter."

But he did wear those vestments; the sisters of St John the Divine provided them for him. He was prepared to acquiesce in the use of these outward signs to demonstrate his respect for the integrity of other people's religious convictions. Sister Lydia writes of his interest in their life and work from 1955 to 1966: "Throughout that period our relationship with him was a strong one, and at all times he showed himself most willing and helpful and supportive of the religious life. His caring understanding showed him to be a true pastor."

For several years Madeleine had suffered from arthritis, an affliction she bore with great fortitude. She insisted on attending everything with Fred although on occasion she was forced to remain seated because of the pain. Early in 1971 she became ill of other symptoms which finally caused her to be hospitalized toward the close of the year. In January 1972 terminal cancer was discovered. Her personal warmth and cheery optimism persisted even in hospital. Back home again she was to continue for some four months in increasing poor health, without a word of complaint. During this time she suffered a stroke. Joan describes it as "really scary" saying, "Father was really wonderful in looking after her." The doctor spoke to Joan about the seriousness of her mother's condition, adding that Fred "doesn't seem to hear us." Joan had the difficult task of trying to explain that his wife had but a short time left, but he did not seem to understand.

On the Victoria Day weekend, Fred brought lunch to the garden. It was a gorgeous day, the garden resplendent with the first blooms of spring. He took her hand saying, "Well, my dear, one day we shall be together in the garden of paradise." They drove out to Edwards Gardens to see the display of flowers there, and in the late afternoon at home again the end came suddenly and peacefully. Fred telephoned the news to me, and within a short time I was with him. For several hours we talked, and he spoke of little endearing things about their life together. Later we drove to the home of his daughter Joan, who with her husband and two children were spending the weekend at their cottage. We waited in the car until they arrived home, when he broke the sad news to them. Archdeacon Dann and myself conducted the funeral service from St Pauls, and Bishop Snell delivered the eulogy. The burial took place in the cemetery on the grounds of St John's, York Mills. Her passing was lamented by all who knew her.

THE GREAT MINISTRY

The day following his wife's funeral Fred Wilkinson chaired a meeting of the Central Review Board of Ontario. In the tradition of his family he could not do otherwise. His sense of duty, combined with his natural energy, enabled him to carry out obligations and take part in public life until the end. This is not to say he was insensitive. Madeleine's death affected him deeply, but this was never outwardly visible. Bert Diltz in the trenches in Flanders in the first World War remembers him "keeping his thoughts to himself."

For more than a quarter of a century he and Madeleine had been alone, Peter and Joan having married and moved away. During this time they had been inseparable; she had been with him in every venture and on all occasions. Now she was gone, and he was truly desolate. He found the emptiness of the house difficult and spent more time with his daughter Joan, persuading her to accompany him to official functions. To her and his closest friends, he confessed his terrible sense of loss and the almost unbearable loneliness. But finally, from his own resilience or as a natural stage of grief, he came to himself and launched out on a new ministry.

One day he began to discuss with me the ministry of music, recounting some experiences he had had over the years, and I suggested he consider giving an organ recital. He replied that he was too much out of practice. But a few weeks later he called to ask how serious I was about the suggestion of a recital. Assured of my intentions he began to appear at St Anne's, where he would practice two or three hours at a time, and on the appointed evening he presented a carefully balanced program to a large audience who gave him a resounding standing ovation. He was very appreciative of the attendance as well as the reception. This was the beginning of a new phase of his retirement years.

He continued to visit the Diocesan Choir School held annually at Trinity College School in Port Hope east of Toronto. He had fostered the birth of this school and had never lost interest in it. One of the senior mentors was Dr Healy Willan, an old friend of long standing and a giant in the musical world. Another was the Reverend Kenneth Scott who with John Bradley was largely responsible for the success of the school. These two men were, along with others, founders of St George's College in Toronto, and great supporters of the bishop. They were extremely kind to him, and during the latter years entertained him on several occasions at a popular resort in New York State.

Fred also launched out on an entirely new pastime. He would invite a small number of people to his home for dinner at which he was both host and cook. Everything was expertly prepared and beautifully served. Dick Newsham observed, "His bravery after Madeleine's death found its best expression when he discovered he loved to cook. 'Now, Madeleine would have done it this way,' he would say." He had of course turned his hand to preparing food before this, but it was usually tea and sandwiches, except for some modest meals during Madeleine's illness. She once told me how she loved the way he prepared scrambled eggs!

He was a plain cook, not a gourmet. He purchased in large quantities and served generous portions; nothing delighted him more than to see guests satisfy hearty appetites. Sometimes a helper, who had come in for other work, would prepare the vegetables, but most often he would do it himself.

Cauliflower, squash, and peas were most often on the menu, and always roasted potatoes, partially boiled first to avoid toughness during roasting! All the vegetables would be perfectly cooked, not tough or mushy. Roast beef was his favourite, and the local butchers would prepare a special cut for him. He served it rare and it was always tender. He would prepare the gravey as well as white sauce for certain vegetables, and all would be served piping hot. His daughter or some other woman would act as hostess, serving the vegetables while he carved the meat. Dessert was simple, usually ice cream with fresh fruit, and coffee was served in the living room. He offered red wine with dinner and martinis before. Once when I arrived early he allowed me to prepare drinks, a rare honour, to his specifications however! No one was permitted to assist in clearing away; this he reserved for himself after the company had left. Once his daughter, my wife, and I washed dishes while he was playing the piano for other guests, and he took us to task when he discovered what we had done.

His guests were from every strata of society and carefully chosen, often with a special purpose. For example, he would be concerned about someone and invite them for dinner where they would meet a colleague in their own field. But most often the only intention for the evening was good food and friendship. The conversation both before and after dinner was spirited and stimulating. Fred always managed to ask a question or make some comment that kept things going. These evenings were imbued with hospitality and old-world charm. I like to call this sort of affair the "Wilkinson Club." George Johnston, a well known publisher and very active layman in the diocese, would from time to time gather a group of men for dinner at the York Club; Fred was always present. Canon Bert Jackson would act as co-host arranging place cards and flowers. Drinks would come first, and then an excellent dinner. Over coffee George would say a word or two referring to someone present, and this would be the first intimation that the person was being honoured that evening. Around the table each in turn would speak to the occasion. In this way, activities that Fred had fostered were often picked up and carried out by those who admired him.

Fred was a Scottish Rite Mason, a Knight Commander of the Order of St Lazarus of Jerusalem, and Grand Prelate of Canada of the Hospitaller Order of the Knights of St John of Jerusalem. According to the latter, "He believes in service over and above the call of duty, and he brought to the order modesty, kindness, and those noble virtues of character which are associated with the ideals of chivalry and Christian service to mankind."

As honourary chaplain of the Canadian Corps of Commissionaires he was faithful in attendance and ready to be of service. The loyal and fraternal associations always tried to ensure his presence whenever possible, particularly on state occasions. Perhaps the last such function he attended was a dinner for the Honourable Pauline McGibbon, retiring Lieutenant-Governor of Ontario. General Legge introduced Fred and brought the guests to their feet in a standing ovation by describing him as "a superb musician, a superb organist, bravest of the brave, the only Canadian to win the Military Medal three times in the first war as a boy who was only eighteen when that war began; above all, a patriot who was a true friend and a true and good bishop."

He derived the greatest pleasure from his association with members of the Royal Canadian Legion in his capacity as honourary chaplain to the Fort York branch of the legion. He spoke of it so much that I became intrigued to the point that he invited me to accompany him to one of their dinner meetings. And so I too became a member! Of all of the organizations to which Fred belonged, the legion occupied first place and gave him great pleasure and comradeship.

At this time of his life, he could more often enjoy recreation with others. Harry Wilson mentions that Fred had never had time for cards prior to retirement, but after this he was persuaded to learn bridge. He didn't play a great deal, but he would occasionally arrive armed with a little book of rules and very obviously enjoyed the challenge of bidding. His great number of evening activities however left him little time for cards. The game that he continued to play up until the end was golf; his enthusiasm for the game never wavered.

In the summer of 1974 a group of men gave Fred a tour of Greece. The memory of his father map's of the journeys of St Paul came alive once more. It was fitting that he should be looked after in such a splendid way, for as Harry Wilson, the organizer of the trip, said, "He never really sought anything for himself, but he was sought out, for he was such a talented fellow." Anyone approaching retirement with dread has but to look at the life of this man and realize what a wonderful and exciting time it can be. Reg Stackhouse agrees with the many who marvel at Fred's activities: "He didn't retire from the human race; he continued to be seen, he continued to be heard, up until the end. He was capable of making new friends, yet he held the loyalty of the old which was evident at the end." Dick Newsham agrees: "He never left anyone behind in his list of friends." He also collected a large number of friends in his later years.

Part of the bishop's charm was his sense of humour. Laman Bruner recalls when he was the preacher at St Martin's in the Field in London. "The church was packed and Fred was in the congregation. With a twinkle in his eye he said, 'I know why the church is packed; I'll show you.' We walked to the front of the church, and on a blackboard Dr Edwards had written 'An American Preacher.' No name was mentioned. Billy Graham was on his first crusade and he was packing the different arenas in England. Any American preacher was considered great."

Fred told the following story in an address to the Toronto Board of Trade. "One cannot recall the years of the war without remembering the tremendous humanity of countless people and their capacity for humour. I remember walking along a very muddy road in a little hamlet called Gouy-Servins with a comrade of mine who had spent five years in Kingston

Penitentiary. As we walked along, the commander of our brigade rode by in a very lordly fashion. He had been the warden of Kingston during the sojourn of my friend. Pointing to him my friend said, "There goes Hughes; you know he and I were in college together'."

Fred enjoyed laughing both with others and at himself. When he and Madeleine stayed at a vast stone edifice in Wales for a few days, he was so cold he put his pyjamas on under his suit. Later in the living room, he noticed his hostess staring at his feet. Looking down he saw the gaudy pyjama legs protruding from under his trousers. Lord Nugent tells this story as it was given to him by Fred and Madeleine.

In August prior to his trip to England, Fred's brother Heber died. He was buried from the cathedral in Hamilton in the Diocese of Niagara, where he had been assistant bishop for some years. Heber had the same shy streak as Fred and the same sense of humour, delighting to tease Fred whenever they were together. There was never any rivalry between them, for typical of the Wilkinson family, each held a deep and lasting affection for the other. Fred's daughter Joan remembers, "Father was very shy and didn't dance. The first time he danced was after he retired." One of these occasions was the marriage of our fifth son Peter. At the reception Fred appeared on the floor with one of two ladies in turn; he moved as though he had been dancing all his life. Gregarious and out going, enjoying the company and fellowship of others, he generally "squired" ladies to functions. For a time after the death of Madeleine it was his daughter Joan who fulfilled this duty. It was not easy for her because of the demands of her own family. Later he escorted one or two lady friends.

One of these was Bertha Houston, the daughter of a Toronto clergyman whom he and Madeleine had known for many years. Her sister Marian had married Minto Swan, a classmate of Freds and a pastor to the armed forces in Kingston, Ontario. Bertha's husband died in 1973, the year after Madeleine; then in 1976 her only son was killed in an air crash. Fred came to see her and was of great comfort. In due time he invited her out to assuage her loneliness as well as his own. It was to be a happy friendship; her outgoing personality was a delight both to Fred and his friends. Once more he decided to go to England, this time accompanied by Mrs Houston. Both of them agonized for some time about the propriety of their travelling together, but family and friends overruled the objections. As Bertha put it, "Our friendship was right and proper. Considering the moral and spiritual background of us both, how could it be otherwise?"

They had a marvellous time seeing old friends. They made a sentimental visit to Ryl in Wales, the camp where Fred spent a considerable time in 1919 before being shipped home, and to St Asaph's Cathedral, the destination of his Sunday walks. Now he motored there accompanied by Mervin Charles-Edwards, retired Bishop of Worcester, his wife, and Bertha. The bishop comments, "He had no false modesty; he had all the confidence of his great gifts. He was a genius and he behaved like one."

Before crossing to France in 1916 Fred was stationed just outside Folkstone. Bertha recalls the return visit. "He was determined to go to Folkstone where he was stationed during the war. That was a strenuous day with a lot of walking; we even walked up to some plateau where a band used to play, all the while Fred recounting how it was in those days." Among those they stayed with during the trip were Lord and Lady Nugent. Lord Nugent praises Fred: "To fill a certain roll, to conduct a military service, if you looked around the world, it would be very difficult to find a man equal to him. He really was in a class by himself."

Fred returned home and admitted finally that he had to have a doctor look at his leg. It had been troubling him before he had gone to England, but he had chosen to ignore it. It was evident to Lord Nugent that there was something wrong with him: "He had some knee trouble when he was last with us, which he resented; he didn't expect to have anything wrong with him." Doctors thought it was a bone problem; Fred thought he had injured his foot playing the organ. It turned out to the phlebitis, and he had to be hospitalized in November of 1979. He was of course a bad patient, chafing at the bit until he was released for convalescence at St Johns Hospital, operated by the Sisters of the church, where of course he was well known. He was amazed at his doctor saying that he hadn't had bacon in years, "Poor fellow." Fred loved his bacon and eggs. Barbara Cody the widow of his late predecessor visited him and had the temerity to suggest that his ministry was now over. He became terribly annoyed with her; he was later to officiate at her funeral! Finally in December he went home. His sister Jean moved into the house and took care of him until, in his resilient manner, he once more became very active. He was always coming from or going to somewhere. During this time Dick Newsham was in the hospital, and Fred visited him every week. Sometimes Fred and I would lunch together. Afterward he might shop for a certain recording he would want, once he had to get a new tie, and in his eighty-fourth year he decided he needed a new cassock.

THE END OF THINGS

While physically the bishop remained as active as before, his illness may have caused him to think about the future. In May 1980 he drew up instructions for his funeral, quoting the writer of Ecclesiastes and adding, "As I shall never know the time of my departure from this earth, I ought to set in order some thoughts with regard to the service of my burial." While of course he did not know, he certainly did have an intimation that seems to come to some people. To paraphrase Professor Haldane, "He felt overtaking him the powers of the world beyond." To Charles Dalton he admitted he was really quite ready to leave. And reflecting on his life to his sister Jean, he quoted the last verse of "When I survey the wondrous cross": "Were the whole realm of nature mine, that were an offering far too small; Love so amazing, so divine, demands my soul, my life, my all," and added, "That sums it all up." During the summer, at a special service at the Royal Canadian Yacht Club amid a beautiful setting, there was rapt attention as he said, "I am now in my eighty-fourth year. I was born by the sea, and although I was never a sailor, everybody needs a pilot." He was no doubt thinking of Harold and the hymn he had played for his brother in England so long ago. At Harold's funeral the first line of the hymn appeared on a purple bordered card sent out after his death in gratitude to his friends: "Jesus saviour pilot me over life's tempestuous sea."

Earlier Bishop Bagnall of Niagara, in conversation with Fred, mentioned that his own ministry would shortly be coming to an end and that there were certain things for which he would always be grateful. "One of them is to have known you and Heber and to number you both among my close friends." Fred leaned over and said, "That is very nice of you to say that, but, if you had known Harold, you would have forgotten all about the two of us. He was worth the two of us; he was by far the best of us." Bishop Bagnall says of Fred, "I was made a bishop in 1949 six years before him, but he was always a father figure to me."

Fred used to quote from the autobiography of Otto Debilius, Bishop of Berlin. The lines surely apply to himself. "I thank God that despite all the changes and upheavals, my life has moved in a straight line. Knowledge and opinions have changed, but my path has remained the same from youth to old age."

On 8 September 1980 he celebrated communion at the marriage of our fourth son. I remember being startled when he began the service; it appeared he had a bad cold, certainly a surprise to me as there had been no evidence of it before. I kept close to him, ready to help, but he composed himself and celebrated as always in his beautiful way. Later in the narthex he said to me, "George Young, what have you done to me this day?" And in answer to my puzzlement he told me he had been deeply moved during the service. I though perhaps it might have been the solemnity of the moment when the bridal couple knelt at the rail to make their communion. But later at his funeral I realized he had chosen the Walmsley tune for the burial psalm, the same tune we had chosen for the nuptial psalm. Whatever the cause it was the first time I had ever seen him emotionally disturbed. But this didn't deter him from having a grand time later at the reception, as he mingled with old friends, calling to me for pincers for the lobster and making sure I asked Bertha to dance. It was to be his last wedding; a few days later he buried the mother of his son-in-law, at which again he seemed deeply moved.

It was 17 September and a beautiful fall day. In the morning he drove to St Clement's Church for what was to be a last rehearsal at that organ preparatory to his recital in St Paul's Church. This of course meant a great deal to him for it was on the organ of St Paul's that he had performed as a very young boy. After rehearsal he drove down to Massey College on the university campus where he collected Mrs Rupert Davies and drove her to Bertha's home. The three of them enjoyed a delightful lunch in the garden. Later he drove home to rest, shower, and change for dinner. He returned to collect the ladies at six and drove the long distance from north Toronto to the Hunt Club in Scarborough. In reminiscing Bertha says, "We had such happy joyous times together." Certainly this was one of them. They remembered the year before when the three of them had been together in England. It was an evening like thousands of others that Fred had arranged. After dinner they retired to the lobby where Fred asked the ladies to wait while he went to fetch the car, telling them he would return in a moment. Thus he walked out into the sunset and eternity.

E'en as he walked that day to God, so walked he from
his birth; in simpleness, and gentleness, and honour,
and clean mirth.

Kipling

ACKNOWLEDGEMENTS

It is with appreciation that I record the following sources whose files were made available to me.

The Globe and Mail
The Toronto Star
The Toronto Sun
The Anglican
The Canadian Churchman
Berkley Divinity School at Yale
Toronto Public Library
The London Gazette March and June 1919
And the Archives of:
Diocese of Toronto, Mrs Hilaray Little
Wycliffe College, Mrs Islay Wilkinson
University of Toronto
Christ Church Dartmouth, Nova Scotia
St Peters Church Toronto
St Pauls Church Toronto
St James Cemetary Toronto
City of Toronto James Fraser
Sisters of the Church Sister Lydia
Awards and Documentation Ottawa
Public Archives Ottawa
Toronto Public Library
Wycliffe College Library, Mrs Lorna Hassell

Dr Stackhouse not only suggested this work but set up a "Wilkinson biographical fund" which assisted with some of the expenses incurred. I am grateful to the following for this tangible support:

G.A. Adamson
Nancy Boxer
Beatrice Heeney
Paul Matthews
A.B. Powell
M. Stevenson
J.C.L. Allen
Richard Boxer
Paul Helliwell
R.S. Malone
W.E. Patterson
David Walker
Ken Andras
John Graham
Bruce Legge
William Oxley
Royal Canadian Legion (Fort York Branch)
Carl Weber

In addition to the public media I am grateful to those good souls who received me into their home, office, or club and cheerfully permitted me to interview them.
Aird, The Honourable John B.
Bagnall, The Right Reverend Walter
Coggan, Lord Donald
Diltz, Dr Bert
Dalton, Colonel Charles
Dann, The Rev. Canon R.P.
Charles-Edwards, The Right Reverend L.M.
Gilling, The Very Reverend Walter
Hilchey, The Venerable Harry

Houston, Mrs Bertha
Hoolihan, Mr and Mrs John (Joan Wilkinson)
Jarvis, Mr Kenneth
Knight, Mr Donovan N.
Langton, Mrs J.M.
Legge, Major General B.J.
Mackintosh, Mr and Mrs D.C. (Lexi Riddell)
Maude, Mr and Mrs Harry
Mowat, Mrs Ruth
Michener, The Right Honourable Roland and Mrs Michener
MacKay, Mrs Pat
Meech, Mr R.G., QC
Nugent, The Lord
Newsham, Mr Richard
Price, Mr Harry
Pocock, The Most Reverend Philip
Richardson, Lloyd
Smith, The Reverand Canon Arthur
Stackhouse, The Rev. Dr Reginald
Snell, The Right Reverend G.B.
Soward, Reginald, QC
Tonkin, Mr Harry
Traviss, Mr James
Walker, Senator David
Weber, Carl
Wiseman, The Reverend Jack
Wilson, Mr and Mrs Harry
Wilkinson, Mr Harold
Young, Captain P.K.

A notice of enquiry in the Canadian Churchman produced a goodly number of correspondents, augmented by a large mailing on my part from which I received replies from all but one.

Correspondents and those interviewed by telephone to whom I am indebted are.

Adam, Mr Gordon England
Brown, The Reverend J. Russell Saskatoon
Brandrick, Mr H.W. Saskatoon
Bruner, Dr Laman H. Loudenville, NY
Bill, Mr E.W. Lambeth Palace, London, England
Clark, The Most Reverend Howard Toronto, Ontario
Calvert, Mrs Kate Calgary, Alberta
Carson, Miss Margaret Toronto, Ontario
Clark, The Very Reverend C.H. New Haven, Connecticut
Clough, The Venerable, J.C. Port Hope, Ontario
Emrich, The Right Reverend Richard S. Sun City, Arizona
Gordon, Mr Walter L. Toronto, Ontario
Hatfield, The Right Reverend Leonard F. Halifax, Nova Scotia
Harrison, Mr J.L. Dartmouth, Nova Scotia
Horsefield, The Ven. R.B. Sydney, BC
Hay, Mrs R. Alan Toronto, Ontario
James, Mrs James L. Brockville, Ontario
Kaye, Mr Peter Vancouver, BC
Kilbourn, Professor William Toronto, Ontario
Lydia, Sister, Toronto, Ontario
Morgan, Mrs H. Richard Brockville, Ontario
MacDonald, Mrs Grace Islington, Ontario
MacDonald, The Reverend Peter S. Dartmouth, Nova Scotia
Molson, Senator Harry Ottawa, Ontario
Marsh, Mrs H.H. Cobourg, Ontario
Nainby, The Rev. Canon W.M. Barrie, Ontario
O'Driscoll, The Very Reverend Herbert Washington, DC
Patrick, The Reverend Barry Calgary, Alberta
Plaut, Rabbi Gunther Toronto, Ontario

Ramsey, Lord Michael England
Ross, Mrs William E. Toronto, Ontario
Renison, Colonel George Toronto, Ontario
Swanson, The Ven. Cecil Calgary, Alberta
Scott, The Reverend Kenneth Toronto, Ontario
Sewell, The Rev. Canon William Hamilton, Ontario
Steer, The Right Reverend Stanley Victoria, BC
Swan, Mrs Marion Victoria, BC
Stokes, The Right Reverend Anson P. Jr. Brookline, Mass.
Taylor, Captain Ray Toronto, Ontario
Wilkinson, Mrs Islay Parry Sound, Ontario
Wiggs, H. Ross Hamilton, Ontario
Watney, The Ven. Douglas Vancouver, BC
Watts, The Rev. Canon L.N. Brampton, Ontario
Wright, The Reverend John Montreal, Quebec
Wilkinson, The Right Reverend T.L. Victoria, BC

Also to Mrs Jean Langton, sister of Bishop Wilkinson, whom I pestered a great deal for information. Her memory and precise details of the early period astounded me, and I cannot begin to thank her enough; also to her sister Mrs Ruth Mowat, who sent me the first letter I received and sat for a lengthy interview. Joan Hoolihan has been supportive and helpful, making available material concerning her father, particularly illustrated material. I am grateful to Professor Diltz for reading the first two chapters, and for his enthusiastic interest; to Lyn Benson for typing the manuscript; and to Margaret Carson, the editor of the *Toronto Anglican*, who provided excellent material from her files over a long period of time; and finally to Jimmy Traviss for his never failing interest, support, and encouragement.

I am grateful to Mr Norman Rathbone for his cover design, to James Barriss and Ted Young Jr for recording equipment, and to Bruce Rathbone, Bursar of Wycliffe College.

APPENDIX

Among some old documents the following two articles had great appeal for me as I am sure they will for the reader.

First is a short Autobiography by Hugh Wilkinson and and dated 16 December 1913. He was the grandfather of the bishop and is remembered by Mrs James when she attended St Paul's in Brockville. "In the front pew always sat old Mr Wilkinson with a group of children from the poorer families of the parish."

Second is a letter dated 4 August 1856 from Ann Wilkinson in England to her son Hugh in Canada. She is of course the bishop's great-grandmother. It is a charming and wise letter from a mother to her son in far off America.

29 Peace St W

Brackville Canada
December 16 . 1913

' a short history of my Life

I. Hugh Wilkinson Was Born at. Mares Field South Side County of Durham England , Post office address, ButterKnowle, My Father Hugh Wilkinson was a fairmer Rented . from the . Duck of Cleavent

Raby Castel, My Mathers name was Ann
Wilkinson thare was, 9, (nine) of, a, famely

Hugh Wilkinson Barn February 16 „ 1834
   Elizabeth „   „   Navembe 4 „ 1835
   Marey   „   „   December 24 „ 1837
   Margret Ann „   Octane 11 „ 1839
   Jane   „   Navembe 26 „ 1841
   William   „   August 31 „ 1844
   Isaac   „   August 3 „ 1846
   Thomas   „   „   Febeuay 15 „ 1849
   Jahn Garge „   „   Jannay 2 „ 1852

J Hugh Wilkinson Left England
an March 26 „ 1856 Came to Liverpool
tuck Pasage an a Saling ship from
Liverpool to New Zork was seven
Weeks and thee days in ariving at
New Zark Praceded to Mantreal
gat Wark at Grand Trunk Railway
Paint. St. Charles assisted to Put
a Pump dawn af No 7 Pear, ar Crib.
to Bild the Pear (the fust Bridge)
after ahaut ane munth. I was
Sent to Lyn to fire a Balase
Engine taking Balase fram Lyn
Balace Pit to Balace the G. T. R
West af Brackville as the G. T. R
was anly apedd far thepack fram Mautied to
                              Brackville

at the Present My famiiley Cansist af
My Wife whase name was Jane Judsan

aff Lyn and 2 Sans Fredrick Wilkinson at the Present Recter of St Peters English Church 190 Carlton St Taronto ant my other San Charles Wilkinson is With P. W. Ellis & Co. 31 Wellington St, Taronto Salsmen (Jauley Manufacbler in the year 1868 I Baugh a Lat an Pearl St Whare I naw Line 50 x 100 ft, had a haus Bilt maned into it in 1873 Whare I naw Line in the year 1887, after nearley 30 years with the Grand Trunk Railway as fitter. I had the affer af the Pasian af master Manack an the Brackville and Westport Railway from R J Harvey who Bilt that Railway and I accepted and Left the G.T.R November 14 x 1887 and started with the Brackville and Westpart an the 15th Remened with that Rade till it was Sald and Lefe an september 10 4 1903 as I was 70 years old I Cancluded to Retike after nearley 50 years Railroadiny I have made faw trips to England since I first Came to Canada, in 1871 I was ane af the first Wimberltan Rifel team af 20 men that was sent to England to Campeto in Rifel Shutten

had my Pasage and Expences Paid
and Recevied 25 Paund in winings
after the matches was aver spent 3
weaks at my Hame Had Bean 16 years
amay then in 1883 I made a trip hame
and in 1884 made a trip hame was
away fram Brockvile ane munth and Had
nine days in England then in 1887 I
made ane mar trip the Last time I was
in England

my father was 91 when he Died My Mathee
was 80 years of age when she at the Present time
I have 2 Brathee and ane Piste Living
in England my Zaungest Bracher Living
an the ald Hame farm whare my father
Lined far aner 50 years

at the Present time I have bean a member
af Sussex Ladge = A & P.A. m Brackvile fae
aner 30 years, Also a member af Brock Lodge
No 9 I.O.O.F far aner 48 years

an February 16th 1914 I will be 80
years af age if I Line till then

                    Mayfield
                      south side
                    Mar Cockfield
                      County, of Durham
                          England
                    May t. 4th 1856

Dear Hugh,
            We have received your letter this
morning, and are very glad to hear that

You are well and getting stouter - that
you are getting on well and have plenty
to do - If you can succeed in getting on
as engine driver it will be a good thing
for you, provided you are steady, civil
attentive and obliging - I am glad to say
that notwithstanding our losses, we are doing
better than could be expected, the crops
of old grass are rather light - seeds are good
and the grain crops are looking well but
rather late - though we have all to work
hard for what we get as you very well know.
We are also very much cheered with the idea
of your sending some money, because
it shews you are getting on well, but
though it would be extremely useful
to us, we do not wish you to put yourself
to any inconvenience.

Your sisters are all very well, your sister
Mary is in a very good place, and Elizabeth
is at Mr. Clark's Barfoot Hall, Margaret Ann
is at Mr. Farrow's, Terrington, and your
father is much in his usual way -
As I write this directly on getting yours
I have not time to get any letters from
your sisters. Wm Lowson and Elliston
are very well, but have not made up
their minds about coming out yet.
I send you my love and best wishes for

your welfare and think you cannot do
better than go to church as often as possible
or to some place of worship on a Sunday,
and work as little as you can on that
day. Let me recommend you also to
read your bible, it will you do good, and
if you attend to it will make you a
wise and good man. Fathers' love.
Hoping to hear from you soon
        I am your affectionate mother
                Ann Wilkinson
and also your affectionate father
                Hugh Wilkinson

I am glad to say we are all ready and we
have got it better together than could be
looked for. Your little brothers are all
very well.

CHRONOLOGY

1896	FHW born, 18 November
1902	Begins the study of music
1904	Wilkinson family move to Toronto
1909	FHW is graduate of Normal-Model School, Toronto
1913	Graduate of Jarvis Collegiate, Toronto
1916	Enlisted with the 10th Canadian Infantry Brigade Signals
1917	Awarded the Military Medal for action at Vimy Ridge
1918	Wounded at Bourlon Wood
1919	Awarded two Bars to the Military Medal
1920	Organist and Choirmaster at the University of Toronto
1922	Received BA in Honour Orientals, University College
	Received MA and Graduated in Theology
	Ordained Deacon, Church of the Ascension, Hamilton in the Diocese of Niagara.
	Married Margaret Madeleine Harkness, 30 September
1924–5	Curate-Assistant, Church of the Ascension, Hamilton

1925	Ordained Priest in St Thomas' Church, Hamilton Born a son, Peter Frederick Francis
1925–8	Professor of Old Testament, Emmanuel College, Saskatoon
1928	BD from General Synod, Church of England in Canada
1929	Born a daughter, Joan Madeleine
1928–32	Rector of St Stephen's Church, Calgary, Alberta
1932–36	Rector and sub-Dean, Christ Church Cathedral, Vancouver, BC
1936–44	Rector of the Church of St James-the-Apostle, Montreal
1939	Major Reserve Chaplain 17th Duke of York Hussars
1944–45	Rector of St Paul's Church, Toronto
1944	Chaplain, Queen's Own Rifles of Canada
1945	DD honoris causa, Wycliffe College, Toronto
1952	Elected coadjutor bishop in the Diocese of Toronto
1953	Consecrated bishop, 6 January DD honoris causa, Trinity College, Toronto
1955	Seventh Bishop of Toronto, 1 July
1956	DD honoris causa, University of Emmanuel College, Saskatoon
1958	LLD honoris causa, University of Toronto Spoke on church unity at Lambeth Conference, England
1959	DCL honoris causa, Bishop's College, Lennoxville, Quebec
1960	Chairman of Ecumenical Affairs, Anglican Church of Canada
1962	Doctor of Sacred Theology, Berkeley Divinity College, Yale University, Hartford, Connecticut.
1963	Host for the Anglican Congress
1965	Co-Chairman of the Anglican-United Church Hymnal Committee

1966	Retired 30 June
	DD honoris causa, Victoria University, Toronto
1967	Chairman, Central Review Board of Ontario
1972	Death of Madeleine Wilkinson
1976	Dinner in honour of 80th birthday at the Military Institute, Toronto
	Bishop Frederick Wilkinson Foundation formed to promote sacred music
1977	Professorship Fund instituted at Wycliffe College in honour of bishops Frederick and Heber Wilkinson
	Honorary Chaplain, Canadian Corps of Commissionaires
	Silver Acorn in Scouting
	Knight Commander of the Order of St Lazarus
	Grand Prelate of St John of Jerusalem
1980	Death of Frederick Hugh Wilkinson, 17 September

INDEX

A

ADAM, Gordon, 55, 59
AFRICA, Churches, 28
AIRD, The Hon John B., 77, 96
AKOMALAFE, Mr, 99
ALBERTA, Province of, 49
ALGOMA, 70, 71
ALLAN GARDENS, 24
AMERICAN CIVIL WAR, 17
AMERICAN, Cities, 20
AMERICAN, Colonists, 17
AMERICAN ORGANIST, 91
AMIENS, City of, 41
ANDRAS, Kenneth, 115
ANGLICAN CHURCH, 48, 90, 106, 112, 115
ANGLICAN CONGRESS 1963, 15, 97, 101
ANGLICAN, The, 81, 93, 105
ANNIE, Laurie, 48
ARCTIC, 71
ARGONAUT ROWING CLUB, 21
ARMRITSAR, Diocese of, 70
ASCENSION, Church of, Hamilton, 50
ATHABASKA, Diocese of, 49, 50, 61
AURELIUS, Marcus, 36
AUSTRIA-Hungary, 29, 30
AUSTRIA-Hungary, Emperor of, 29

B

BACH, JS, 69, 92
BAGNALL, The Rt Rev Walter, 75, 78, 84, 85, 100, 128
BALKAN WAR, 29
BARFOOT, The Most Rev Walter, 52
BARING-GOULD, The Rev Sabine, 28
BARRIE, City of, 73
BATTLE OF BRITAIN SERVICE, 92
BEETHOVEN, L.V., 39, 108
BELGIC, S.S., 43
BELGIUM INVADED, 30
BELL TELEPHONE, 45
BELLINGHAM, Washington, 56
BERKLEY DIVINITY SCHOOL, Yale University, 106
BERLIN, City of, 30, 91
BEVERLEY, The Rt Rev Alton Ray, 70, 71
BICKERSTETH, Burgon, 91
BIRKINSHAW, R.C., 98
BISLEY, Canadian team at, 30
BOSTON MARATHON, 20
BOSWELL, 10
BOTHWELL, The Rev William, 93
BOURLON WOOD, Flanders, 42
BRADLEY, John, 120
BRAMSHOT, England, 34
BRANDON, Bishop of, 52
BRITAIN, 17, 32, 84